Land of the Deer

The Road to Drumnafunner

A Journey through North-East Scotland

Robert Smith

BIRLINN

First published in 2007 by
Birlinn Limited
West Newington House
10 Newington Road
Edinburgh EH9 1QS

www.birlinn.co.uk

ISBN 13 978 1 84158 506 2
ISBN10 1 84158 506 8

British Library Cataloguing-in-Publication Data
A catalogue record for this book is available from the British Library

Typeset by Carolyn Griffiths
Printed and bound by Cromwell Press, Trowbridge, Wiltshire

AE

CONTENTS

ACKNOWLEDGEMENTS

I met many friends and helpful folk on the road to Drumnafunner. Their stories filled these pages and I am grateful to them.

I would also like to thank the 'backroom squad' who provided pictures and information. Among them were members of my family, and my friends Alistair and Evis Ritchie, who tramped the tracks to help dig out the secrets of this North-east corner.

I salute them all!

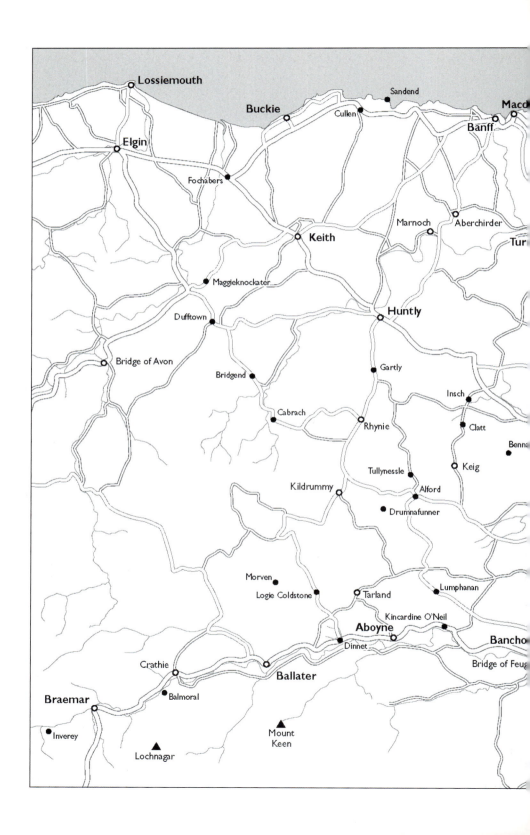

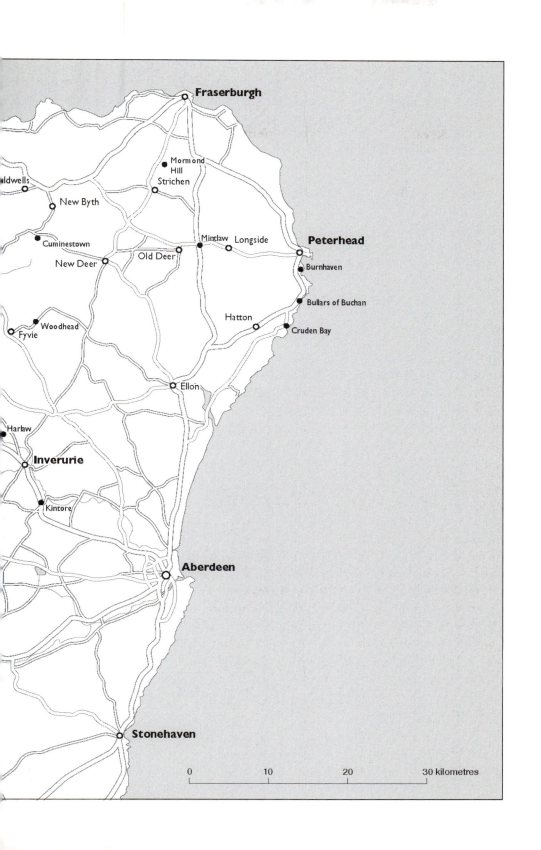

Fraserburgh

Mormond Hill

Strichen

ldwells

New Byth

Cuminestown

New Deer

Old Deer

Mintlaw   Longside

Peterhead

Burnhaven

Bullars of Buchan

Hatton

Cruden Bay

Woodhead

Fyvie

Ellon

Harlaw

Inverurie

Kintore

Aberdeen

Stonehaven

0   10   20   30 kilometres

INTRODUCTION

Fin God made Buchan flat and gweed
He'd nowt and corn in his heid
popular saying

Anumber of my forbears pleitered around the nowt and corn that God had in his heid when he made Buchan. They were scattered about Mormond Hill like bees round a byke. They weren't all farmers, though. I had an uncle, William Cockburn, who was a souter at Mintlaw, and another who mended tackety boots at Lonmay.

Up on Brucklay Estate another uncle, Alec Murdoch, was grieve at Shevado Farm, and over at Cauldwells, near New Byth, were the Cummines. Jimmy Cummines, my cousin, wasn't too happy about toonsers coming out from Aberdeen for free meals. He made us work for them by hoein neeps. My father was brought up on a farm in the Cruden area and had his share of howkin turnips, and after the First World War, in which he served with the Gordons, he went into Aberdeen to become a bobby.

There were cousins of mine scattered all over Buchan – vets and doctors and pharmacists and schoolteachers – but I rarely saw them. Sandy Murdoch, the Brucklay grieve's son, left his chemist's shop in Mintlaw and went off to a fishing toun on the Banffshire coast. He was a railway buff and we occasionally met and exchanged solemn thoughts on the Buchan puffers. With all these relatives planting their roots in Buchan I was always drawn back to it.

Peter Buchan, the fisherman poet from Peterhead, liked to think of himself as a Burnhaven man. He said he was 'half Burnie' because his father was born and bred in Burnhaven, a village that had a reputation for telling tall tales – 'binders'. He wrote a poem about it:

It seems to the truth ye're a stranger,
I'm gaun by the binders ye tell;
But it's a' richt wi' me,
Tho' ye come we a lee,
For I'm mair than half Burnie masel.

I remember thinking when I read this that with the links I had with Buchan I would be entitled to claim that I was 'half Buchan'. This book takes you to Buchan, but it spreads far beyond it to the lands 'flat and gweed', to the 'grim hills and the green', the muckle hills which the poet J.M. Caie said were like warriors flinging a challenge to man, and the little hills, couthy and kindly. It probes south to the Angus Glens, north to *Hamewith* country at Alford, on to Aberdeen, and Deeside, and over the sea to the Orkneys and the Shetland Isles.

It is a book about the myths of these places, their legends, their rivers and glens, and it is also about the people who have lived there, about the communities that have grown around them. It is set against a tapestry of works by North-east writers like Caie, Murray and Milne, and of course women poets like Mary Symon and Violet Jacob. The starting point is Drumnafunner, where the Donald family lived and from where the poet Charles Murray walked over the moors to school. Here, up on Reekie Brae, you can learn the strange story of the Witch's Cairn. There are many other intriguing places, such as the Glen of Horses, and Kinkers, and you can read about the first travellers who came to Scotland and met the 'Wild Scots'.

1
THE FUNNER

The road to the farm at Drumnafunner runs through Hamewith country. It isn't much of a road, just one of those countless farm tracks that trail across the face of the North-east. The farm of Drumnafunner is no great distance from the school where Charles Murray went 'wi' his beuks an' his skaalie and slate'. It is a strange, tortuous name – Drumnafunner – and I half expected to see it in one of Murray's poems. But another name took priority: Hamewith, the road that's never dreary.

'Hamewith' meant homeward. 'West ower Keig,' wrote Murray, 'stands Callievar wi' a' the warl' to me atween.' Here, there are roads that spin away in all directions – to the Glen of Horses, to the Tree of Gold, and the village of Kinkers. I followed a road that took me to Droustie's in search of the Wild Warlock, and I searched for a Kebbock Steen in Buchan.

But it was Murray who started it all, for he showed me people and places I might never have known. He led me to the Funner, and to little Nan. Murray's poetry floats over the Howe of Alford like the 'win' cairtit clouds'. Wherever you go there are reminders of his early years in Alford. This is sheep country and Murray walked on the bare moors and knew the people who lived in remote sheep farms with names like Tibberchindy and Badens and Drumnafunner. He wrote about their lives, about winter in the Howe, and the coming of spring, when the sheep were 'aff to the hills again as hard as the lambs are able'. He wrote, too, about the couthy Packman, who 'humpit roon the countryside' spreading his ferlies [wonders] out on kitchen floors – 'thummles, needles, preens an' tape for whip-the-cat to wale' [tailor to choose].

The name Drumnafunner – *Druim na conaire* – means 'the ridge of the path or way', but it is difficult now to find these old ways in the heather. It was also known as 'the ridge of the kennel'. There was a house on the Drumnafunner ridge at one time, but it has long since gone. The Donalds lived there: Tom Donald the shepherd, his wife and their family of twelve – 'seven loons and five quines'.

Back in the 1920s, Murray and his friend Captain Cook of Asloun, the local laird, were on a Sunday stroll after attending the kirk, and they called in at Drumnafunner. Tom Donald met them and with him was little Nan, his daughter. Captain Cook tapped her on the shoulder and pointed to his companion. 'This is the man who makes all those poems you get at the school,' he said.

Nan, as she told me, was unaware that the poet at her side once sat in one of those desks in the school. He was a pupil there and in a letter to his teacher, Anthony McCreadie, he wrote, 'The old Gallowhill days crowd back. I can see the gean trees, the hedge, the dyke and the well and I can see Sandy Anderson of Westside harrying [robbing] a bike on top of one of Adam Taylor's dykes.'

I thought that Gallowhill was a strange name for a school. It made me wonder if the bairns sat at their desks thinking about bodies swinging on a

The old farm at Drumnafunner, home of the Donalds

gibbet up on the hill. Well, it didn't seem to bother young Charlie Murray. Maybe he was preoccupied with the sound of a wee herd's whistle:

The feet o' ilka man an' beast gat youkie when he played –
Hae ye ever heard o' whistle like the wee herd made?

Through Murray's poetry the sound of that whistle carried a long way beyond the Howe. In his book *A Search for Scotland* R.F. Mackenzie, Aberdeen's controversial headmaster, recalled travelling in a guard's van at the tail end of a mixed train between Inveramsay and Insch at the other side of Bennachie from Murray's Alford. 'The guard recited "The Whistle",' he wrote, 'his eyes shining, glee in his voice as we stotted round corners and he steadied his stance by holding on to the brake lever, but never for a moment losing his lilt of the poem.'

Little Nan, now in her nineties, told me about Drumnafunner and the Donalds. She was born on 8 August 1914. She is a widow now, and has a mind as sharp as a pin and a memory to match it. She put me right about

The Donald family, 1963 (Bob, Archie, Tom, Davy, Will;
Jim, Mary, Belle, Betty, Elsie, Nan, George)

the name Drumnafunner, which is a bit of a tongue twister. 'We aye ca'd it the Funner,' she said, and from then on I called it the Funner. Her father was one of seven sons and he himself had seven sons. 'Nearly a' the family was ca'd efter uncles,' she said. She did a rollcall for me on the loons and quines: Mary, Jim, Tom, Davy, Belle, Archie, Bob, Will, George, Elsie, Betty and Nan herself, who was also known as Annie.

Life on the Drumnafunner hill was never easy, but it was never dull. Feeding this large family was a major effort. They made soup in a boiler during the week, but on Fridays they got a treat: cocoa instead of soup. They had a kind of Pony Express operating between Alford and the Funner. The Alford grocer had two Shetland ponies and they were used to carry food and other necessities up the hill to the Funner and to Tibberchindy and Badens. The farms' orders were taken down by the postie on Friday and the Shetland ponies were loaded up and sent off up the hill with two of the grocer's sons.

They went first to Badens, which was one of a number of so-called 'second places' used as overnight 'halts' when driving sheep. Here, sheep and dogs were rested for the night. Charles Murray mentions Badens in a poem called 'Jeames', which is about a lad who was too fond of the 'yill' [ale] and found himself in trouble on his way home from the Scuttrie Market. He fell among the glaur at 'Muggart's door' [Muggarthaugh Inn], forgot his 'shaltie' [Shetland pony] and 'stoitered aff alane, he kent nae whaur, an' sleepit wi' the sheep on Baadin's hill'.

There was no road to Badens. Nan's direction to it was 'owre the hill and through the heather'. The only road from Drumnafunner was the road to Asloun, with its eighteenth-century house and the remains of Asloun Castle, where Montrose spent the night before the Battle of Alford.

Sheep were scattered about the hill when I was there and I asked Nan if her father had had a lot of them to look after. She said he had, and he also had sheep of his own – and he got twins from them. Tom always said that the shepherds' sheep 'aye got twins'. The Donalds were proud of their reputation as shepherds. I was told the story of a teacher who talked to her class about Jesus as the Good Shepherd. Later, she tested them by asking, 'Who was the Good Shepherd?' Up shot one pupil's hand. 'Please, miss,' he said, 'Robbie Donald was the good shepherd.'

The Donalds were at the Funner for twenty years, then three 'flittings' came, one after the other. A man came to the Funner to work on the farm, but the cottar house wasn't big enough for him and his family so Tom said he would move to let him into the farmhouse. That first move took Tom to

Dubston at Tullynessle, the second to Logie Newton, and his third move took him back to the Funner. It happened when the shepherd who had replaced him at Drumnafunner retired. His job was advertised in the papers and Nan's father applied for it, although he thought he would be regarded as too old – he was fifty-eight. He got the job and it was back to the Funner for the Donald family.

We spoke about Nan's neighbours, about the folk at Badens 'ower the hill' and at Tibberchindy, north of the Funner. They were sheep folk like the Donalds and when the Tibberchindy shepherd visited them on one occasion he found that the Donalds had a new 'toy' in their house.

'We had a wireless that hung on the wa',' Nan explained.

'A crystal one?' I asked.

'No, nae a crystal een,' said Nan. 'We werna as bad as that.'

The Tibberchindy shepherd was impressed by this new technology. He stood looking at this wonderful box on the wall and finally said 'Imagine hearing that a' the wye fae London.'

Memories came back as we sat in her house in Alford and spoke about the old days at Funner. She told me about Archie Coutts, an uncle of her father's, who was a dominie at Glen Gairn. 'The bairns a' had to tak' a peat to the fire there,' she said. She laughed at the memory of the local minister who always carried a supply of sweets in his pocket. When he made a pastoral visit to Drumnafunner he would always bring sweeties for Daisy. No, Daisy wasn't one of the Donalds – she was the family cow. Daisy and the minister walked about the farm, side by side, as if they were lifelong friends.

Frank McLean, who came from Maggieknockater – a place I wrote about in my last book – were cousins of the Donalds, and came to Drumnafunner for their holidays every year. There were five loons with them one year, and Nan recalled how they were walking down the hill when Frank's wife said, 'Look, there's five sheep gaun aboot the hooses.'

'Sheep?' said Frank. 'There's nae sheep there.'

'Ken fit it wis?' said Nan. 'The five loons took aff a' their claes and were runnin' aboot naked.'

It didn't cause much of a scandal – the folk who lived in the shadow of Callievar had seen worse than that. Callievar is not much of a hill, less than two thousand feet in height. In 1887 the Donside folk built a monster fire on the hill to celebrate Queen Victoria's Jubilee.

There is a whiff of brimstone in the dark corners of Callievar. 'Auld carlins [women] ride on their brooms astride, awa' thro' the midnight air,' wrote Charles Murray. As far as I know, Murray never raked the murky world of witches and warlocks for his poetry, but he did write a poem called 'The Witch o' the Golden Hair':

Fae the earth she's reived, fae the Heav'n she's thieved,
For her cauldron's deadly brew.

I have sometimes wondered if Murray's witch was prompted by the curious story of Meggie Stott, an old woman, branded as a witch, who wandered the moors near Gallowhill where Murray went to school. It was Nan who told me about Meggie, and the Witch's Cairn on Reekie Brae too. Meggie had a cruel end. She was stealing meal at a meal girnal in Asloun when the head of the girnal came down and killed her – 'hanged her,' said Nan.

They said that a witch had to be buried between two lairds' lands and in sight of a mill and a kirk, and the only place they could find was up on Reekie Brae. They built a cairn to mark the spot and folk passing it always added a stone to it. 'There were nae steenies on the road because it wisna lucky to pass Meggie Stott's without adding a stone to the cairn marking her burial place,' said Nan. 'Naebody would have missed doing it.'

The cairn had been kept for years and years, said Nan. Everybody put a stone on it. But all that changed. Nan told me how she had folk up from England and she said she would take them to Reekie Brae. 'I was tellin' them about Meggie and the cairn but they had done something to the road,' said Nan. 'I think they'd been takin' doon trees. I looked and looked and looked and couldna see Meggie's cairn. Then someone said, "That's the cairn"; there was jist a heap o' little steenies.'

The workmen had little concern for an old cairn stuck at the roadside and their machinery drove over it, pushing it into the bank. Now, only a part of the Witch's Cairn stands on Reekie Brae – and over the hill only part of the Funner remains. When Captain Cook retired, Lawson's of Dyce took over Drumnafunner. The cottar house slates were taken away to re-roof the eighteenth-century house of Asloun and the house itself was demolished. In the end, all that remained on the 'ridge of the kennel' were a few outbuildings.

Nan regretted the wiping out of her old home. 'The house was a good house,' she said. As for the outbuildings, she remembered names that had been carved on the thrashing mill. Now that they are gone a little bit of history has been lost. But one part of the old house still remains – the floor. In the early days there was a clay floor in the house, but the Donalds decided to have something better – a concrete floor.

Nan told me that the man who came to lay the new floor said he had never seen such an out-of-the-way place, adding that he would have to make a good job to save himself coming back to it. Well, the house has gone, but the concrete floor sits there in gloomy isolation, almost as if waiting for someone to come back and build another house around it.

Not many folk nowadays know about the Funner or about Meggie Stott and what happened to her. She is forgotten, just like the carlins riding their brooms on Callievar. But the Witch's Cairn beckoned me and I made a trip to Reekie Brae to see it – and maybe to throw a last 'steenie' on Meggie's grave. After all, it would be bad luck to ignore it.

Nan, that incomparable lady who shrugged off her years until it was as if

Nan on Reekie Brae

she was half her age, was our guide. We drove to the bottom of Reekie Brae and parked our car at Reekie Farm, where Noreen Insh, from Renfrew, lives with her husband George, who was away on an oilrig. The brae climbs steeply away from the farm, a rutted, stony track that can take only heavy traffic. 'Where's Drumnafunner?' I asked Nan as we puffed up the brae.

'Ower the ither side of the hill,' said Nan.

I realised then that the route we were taking was the one Nan had followed every day on her way to school at Gallowhill – a two-mile walk, four miles there and back. Reekie Brae actually went over the hill and down to Tibberchindy, which had been a fair-sized farm at one time. There was no road linking Drumnafunner to the Tibberchindy road, so Nan had had to go through the heather at the start of her walk to school. Every day she had passed the Witch's Cairn and thought nothing about it. She had often put a 'steenie' on it herself.

Up and up we went and every time we stopped for a breather Nan said, 'It's nae far noo.' The OS map showed the track going over Craig Hill, giving its height as 361 feet, which seemed a trifle, but it wasn't an easy walk. I wondered how the brae came to be known as Reekie; perhaps it

Nan at the Witch's Cairn

had something to do with the days of peat fires. In old records it was given as Rickie.

Names can be interesting, but confusing. We reached an opening into a field and Nan said we were at the Leg o' Mutton. It sounded like the name of a cafe, but the field was called Leg o' Mutton because of its shape. In those days, all the fields were given names; now they get numbers or nothing at all.

When we found the Witch's Cairn I remembered the old saying that a witch had to be buried between two lairds' lands and in sight of a mill and a kirk. I asked Nan if you could see them from here and she pointed them out – the lairds' lands at Asloun and Breda, the kirk and where there had been a meal mill at Annfield, south of Breda.

Near the top of Reekie Brae we came on a large heap of stones at the side of the road, piling up on the bank. 'That's it!' said Nan. The cairn had been pushed hard into the bank. Its shape was barely definable, but there was little doubt that it was the cairn. In time, the stones will fall away and there will be nothing left to remind us of Meggie Stott, who died trying to get a bite to eat from a meal girnal.

I sat at the Witch's Cairn and tried to imagine what it had looked like. Nan told me that it had been about 5 feet high, with a broad base. The 'steenies' that folk had dropped on to it had strengthened it. Not long before it was struck by the road workers' vehicle a woman came to the cairn and tidied it up, then cut the grass around it. I like to think that she will come back again, with other helpers, and will rebuild the Witch's Cairn, with a plaque beside it to tell of how Meggie Stott lived and died in this corner of Hamewith country.

I was the last to leave the Witch's Cairn. I could see the others well down the brae – my friends Doug and Mary, who had toiled up the hill with me; my wife Sheila, who had reached the cairn and was going back down the brae with Nan. It is unlikely that Nan will climb Reekie Brae again, as she admitted, but she will remember the time that she climbed to see the Witch's Cairn four days before her ninety-first birthday.

2
THE FORGOTTEN GLEN

The Felagie Burn – feith leaghaidh, 'the slow burn' – wanders lazily through the lands of Aberarder, past the ruins of forgotten settlements, past the remains of the Crofts of Balnoe and the old kirk at Knockan, and on to join the Fearder burn as it tumbles down from Auchnagymlinn, a place long extinct, where the grave of a giant was said to lie in the forking of the burn.

This was a forgotten glen which once had a school with 128 pupils – 88 boys and 40 girls. It also had a chapel, a burial ground, and bonnet lairds of its own. I had walked along the Felagie track with an old friend, Donald Grant, now dead. I remember how we stood on a loading bay for timber that had been cut out of the moor. There was a lone birch tree beside a dyke – a 'birkie'. 'I want to be buried here,' said Donald.

The ashes of his mother and father, his sisters and his Auntie Nell had been scattered in the glen. It turned out that we were standing on the site where Auntie Nell's cottage had been. It had been razed to the ground by the laird of Invercauld, set on fire and swept away by bulldozers. There was nothing to show that anyone had ever lived there.

Donald's father was host at the Inver Inn in the 1920s and young Donald spent his holidays with his Auntie Nell (Helen Bain) in the 'hoosie' at Milton of Aberarder. When his father moved to the Grant Arms in Fochabers in 1932 he still went on holidays to Aberarder. He swam in the Felagie Burn, tramped the glen from end to end – he lost his dog in the bogland – and watched the red deer come down from the hills to be fed. They were, he told me, the best days of his life.

The Grants were well known on Deeside. Francis Grant, young Donald's grandfather, lived in the Fungle at Aboyne and was gamekeeper to Dr William Cunliffe-Brooks on Glentanar Estate. His son, Donald Kennedy Grant, senior, born in 1885, was a fee'd loon in Glen Cat and when he grew up ran a grocer's shop in Aberdeen. In 1920 he took over the Inver, or the Inver Crathie Hotel as it was called then. He later took over the Seafield Hotel in Cullen.

Young Donald's mother, Annie, and her sister, Auntie Nell, were both employed at Balmoral Castle in the service of Queen Victoria. They worked alongside many of the Indian servants brought to Balmoral by the Queen, including the notorious Munshi Abdul Karim. 'They were skivvies,' said Donald, who thought they were poorly treated.

'Wee Donald' was the Grant I knew well. He had made contact with me about an article I had written, and often came with me on forays into Deeside. He ran a garage at Cullen and later became the owner of two shops, and he worked as a ghillie at Glentanar after he retired. His home was in Cullen and he had a cottage at Inchmarlo, and spent a lot of time there.

Donald often put me in touch with stories of events and people on Deeside, but the most interesting tale came in a manuscript he gave me. It was written in an old cash notebook and the author was his father, who had called it a 'short story on the life of Donald Kennedy Cameron Grant, born on 25 January 1885'. Old Donald never completed his autobiography, but what he wrote provided a fascinating glimpse of life on Upper Deeside at the tail end of the nineteenth century and in the early years of the twentieth century.

Donald Kennedy Grant, who was fee'd as a herd lad in Glen Cat for the sum of three pounds for six months, described the meals laid on for farm workers. Porridge, oatcakes and milk were obviously the essential foods for brosy ferm loons. Milk was put in bowls at night after 'the six milking,' then the kettle was left at boil. You made your own meal brose, taking the cream from the top of the milk. The men took a quarter of oatcakes and the rest of the milk was left in the bowl.

Donald left a culinary hint I had never heard of until I read his manuscript. He said that the porridge was always well boiled, but before pouring he added one or two handfuls of meal. You had to eat your porridge at once in the old days, otherwise you had to use a knife to cut it.

The following is an extract from Old Donald's diary:

My second was on the same hill at 4 am. Had seen him the night before so went out at daybreak. It was also very difficult to get a proper stance to fire from as the only place suitable you could see the stag was from a steep slope through the trees. The shot had gone a little left, but right on the chest. This turned out to be the finest head, the horns 14 point, perfect shaped, called Imperial.

At Inver you had to protect your crops from deer, hares and rabbits . . . in fact, the rabbits were the best paying animal on the farm. Had also got leave from the gamekeeper to shoot the game on the hill to save him carrying the rabbits.

I leased the Inver Crathie hotel in 1920. I had just four horses, three milk cows, hens, ducks and one hotel lodger, but had the wife, her mother and Aunt Nell and of course wee Donald [his newly born son] within a short time. So my farming and hotel life began. The horse had to be disposed of and two good ones bought. They were very expensive then, a good one over £100, but I made a good buy as I had both for my whole time at Inver.

Previously, the crop had been badly destroyed by deer. I took care the deer did little damage; in fact, we had always had a little venison for own use. It had not then become fashionable as a hotel meal. I had, in fact, shot two stags with a .303 rifle brought back from S. Africa. My first was a perfect shot when I was moving up the hill on a poaching expedition. The stag was on the skyline and because of rocks I could not get nearer than at least 500 yards. Anyway, after firing he disappeared. So I went up and to my surprise found it dead.

The hotel trade in Old Donald's early days was 'pretty poor', largely because there was only one bus a day carrying passengers to and from the Ballater trains. This bus also carried the mail to Crathie and Braemar, where it was delivered by a postman or by women. The postman was out on his rounds one day when he met Queen Victoria at Corndavon Lodge, a shooting lodge on the north side of the Gairn. During their conversation the Queen, who was out with a shooting party, asked how long it would take him to cycle from one point to another and he replied, 'Twal meenits full out.' The Queen thought he was foreign and asked the gamekeeper what he meant. She was told it was twelve minutes as fast as he could go.

The diary goes on to comment on the hard work on the farm. Old Donald managed without a ploughman and in fact won a prize for

The ruins of Aberarder School

'plowing'. He also made the lunch for the competitors, using a boiler which was kept for making hen or pig meat. The stew was made from venison gifted by Balmoral or Invercauld.

The school, with 128 pupils, closed because it became impossible to get teachers. Old Donald was given the contract to drive the pupils to Crathie school, at first with what he called a brown [a brown horse] brought from Braemar Castle, which had to face 'snow and ice and the storms, then mere mud, worse than snow, sometimes 18 inches deep.' The diary goes on:

> Had got to know most of the gamekeepers so had lots of stalking and lots of funny experiences on the hills. Once got lost in the fog. The gamekeeper had come away without his compass. We had seen some hinds but were on the wrong side for the wind so made to get to the other side of the hill. On arriving there we had got across our tracks and arrived in a sheltered spot. We stopped for a conference so I produced a bottle of rum which brightened all.
>
> I told them I had made up my mind to face the wind and keep direct into it until I came to the road. We all went and in a small time came on a small tree which the keeper knew. He said we must be very near the deer and it

proved so and we shot three. The next trouble was to get them over the Cluny burn. The stones had ice on top and I had to get in the water. Once in the van we were soon in Braemar where the kettle was soon full of hot stout and rum, and a pair of dry socks. That days outing was in Glencallater.

The keeper at Glen Cluny gave Old Donald permission to walk there when the shooting tenant was absent. When Donald took up the invitation the keeper said he couldn't come because he was going south to Nottingham to give a demonstration of curing deer. 'Even a keeper can learn the English a few tips,' said Donald. It was arranged that the ghillie or pony man would accompany him, but Donald 'met him on his way to Braemar and the pub so knew he would not see him again that day'. Donald went on by himself and ended up having what he called 'one of the sporting days of my life'.

Old Donald described in his diary how he came on a lot of stags 'but they were out of season and knew it and did not move'. Farther on he came upon a hind and calf. The calf had seen him but not the hind. 'The calf had given the mother no peace after it had seen me,' he wrote, 'how

Ruined lodge on Invercauld Estate

soon does Nature take note.' He moved up the hillside and came on a 'nice lot – 15 to 20, shot two dead and wounded another'. The wounded deer did a dive into a burn and Old Donald shot it again.

Up in the Slugan Glen on the Invercauld Estate there is a ruined lodge where hillwalkers often take shelter. I have been in it many times and had heard the story that was told in Old Donald's diary. He said an Invercauld lady had been sent to the Slugan lodge to have a child to one of the gardeners. Donald's description of her as 'an Invercauld lady' bears out what was said at the time – that the pregnant woman was someone of high rank.

Old Donald began to take an interest in salmon fishing. One Sunday he cycled up by the River Dee with 'the garden fly' [worms] and a 'penny book'. He caught one salmon, landing it after a struggle. 'How proud I felt,' he wrote. Later, he often went poaching with a local ghillie from Inver as his guide. There was no fishing rod, just a cycle lamp and a gaff. One keeper he knew had a dog that went after the fish in the burns. It went into the water, drove them up to the top of the pool, then fixed one by the tail and took it out. 'Had a very exciting night,' wrote Old Donald. 'Plenty of fish and gallons of booze to keep the cold out. It seemed to be an annual event and the party knew where the bailiffs were.'

When Old Donald bought the Grant Arms Hotel in Fochabers he had no land attached to it, but he kept pigs. They were, he said, 'very fond of beer. We always gave them the bottom of the beer barrel which contained hops.' He was never very fond of Fochabers folk. 'A great number were retired teachers and would-be toffs who went to Elgin for their drink so the locals would think they were TT.' After seven years at the Grant Arms he heard that Cullen, which had been 'dry' for eighteen years, had gone 'wet'. The Seafield Arms was on the market and he bought it. He then sold his Cullen hotel after the Second World War and worked as a ghillie on various estates. This is what he wrote in his diary:

I've had a gent who fished for three or four days and caught nothing. His wife on the same beat had had a few, so one day when he had stuck his boat in the river and his fly up near the top of a tree we had a few words. He told me he had fished since boyhood and demanded to know why his wife and others were getting fish and he none.

'Just tell me why!' He said.

'Well, sir,' I said, 'ye canna fish.'

I remember thinking when I read Old Donald's response that it was the kind of remark his son would have come up with. Young Donald, who flew with the RAF during the Second World War, was a chip off the old block. He was something of a gallus character, unabashed by officialdom, not afraid to speak his mind. Like his father, he knew many of the ghillies and keepers, and worked with them from time to time. He was not averse to a bit of poaching, like his father. He often took me into places the lairds would have frowned on. His heart was always in Aberarder, where he had roamed the hills and moors and stayed in his Auntie Nell's 'hoosie'.

There are many reminders of old Aberarder hidden in this forgotten glen. Wherever you go you come upon them: ruins like the gaunt skeleton of the school on the road to Milton which in 1810 had 128 pupils but not enough teachers to keep it going; or the old kirk, now a private house, with a new church bell to replace the one that had mysteriously disappeared. I remember Donald pointing to a ruin on the hill above the school. There had been a smiddy and a croft there and it was thought that it was where Margaret Leys, John Brown's mother, had lived.

Aberarder Church is now a private house

There were buildings crumbling away out of sight behind old moss-covered dykes as if they were concealing their broken walls from the winds and storms that blew over the hills around them. I had often tramped down the road to the Queen Mother's cottage at Auchtavan without knowing that behind the dyke leading to it were the remains of an old settlement, ruin after ruin, set high on the brae.

Jock Esson was a shepherd at Auchtavan – the last person to live and work in what became the Queen Mum's howff. Donald Grant knew Jock well. He often got a cup of tea from him, out of a bowl, said Donald, a white bowl in the old-fashioned way. Farther on was Auchnagymlinn, which was the highest farm in the glen. It was washed away in the Muckle Spate of 1829, leaving only a trickle of stones and the fanciful tale about a giant.

There were other settlements, like Balloch and Knockan, but it was down by the Felagie Burn that Donald recalled the past. I was standing with him on the site of Auntie Nell's house when he spoke bitterly about how the laird had razed her house. 'Don't forget the Clearances!' said the caption to a picture in his photograph album.

The album showed what was left after the bulldozers had done their worst: a heap of stones that was Bella Catnoch's house – 'what they left of it,' said the caption; the shell of Maggie Lamont's house, with its 'winky' window, and another abandoned house where tinkers had stayed. On the south side of the Felagie Burn there had been a group of houses known as Felagie Village, but all that remained of it was a number of barely visible foundations.

I have never forgotten that last visit to Aberarder with Donald Grant. I still remember him standing in that timber bay stirring the dust with his foot as if he could rub out what had been done to Auntie Nell's house, or for that matter, to the glen. It was my last time with him at Aberarder – and I have never discovered whether or not his ashes were scattered beside the 'birkie' tree.

3
THE GRISLY GHOST

The village of Woodhead lies about a mile to the east of Fyvie. It is a quiet, scattered community, said by the writer Nigel Tranter to be

All Saints Episcopal Church, Woodhead

Fyvie Parish Church (the Established Church)

'over-churched'. When I took myself there I discovered that the years had changed all that. There is a large Established church – Fyvie Parish Church. It had been a magnificent church at one time but now it has a weary air of neglect. I discovered that services are still held there twice a month – the congregation usually totalling about half a dozen. And there is the Episcopal Church of All Saints, 1849. The Free church is now disused and in a state of disrepair. Then there was St Mary's Church, which I was told was 'lost'. They said it had been 'under All Saints'. But if All Saints and St Mary's were both on the same site, why was the graveyard not more extensive?

Just south of the village the Ythan weaves its way through a series of deep winding dens, flanked by the Braes of Minonnie. The dens have quaint names like the Clattie Den, the Den of Crichie, the Little Den – and the Den of Dennilair. The Den of Dennilair is an idyllic spot, but there was a time when people shied away from it as if it carried the plague. According to an old poem the bravest and boldest avoided Dennilair:

Oh, wordly wild in Dennilair!
The bravest, boldest dinna care

To wanner, e'en mid noon-tide's glare,
Doon by its stream;
Though fair the flowers that deck its braes,
And blythe the birds that lilt their lays,
Nae sweet-faced bairns there mak' their plays,
Or happy dream.

The reason no sweet-faced bairns played in that ravine below Woodhead was because it was the haunt of a ghost. Fyvie Castle had its ghost, and in the great arch above the entrance it had its meurtriere, or 'murder hole', where molten lead was poured down on the heads of invaders. But Dennilair had a far more sinister hole – 'the hole where the grisly ghost lay'.

There have been at least three versions of this ghostly tale. The story of this apparition was first told in 'The Grisly Ghost of Bairnsdale', an old long-forgotten ballad that in December 1872 was sent to *Scottish Notes and Queries* by a Dr Nicol of Alford. He hoped that the publication would preserve it. He said it had never been in print before and he attached a note from John Forbes, Mains of Fyvie Cottage, who was said to be 'its original transcriber'.

Forbes said the ballad was taken down by his wife 'from the lips of her grandmother, Mrs Greig', at Sunnyside, Fyvie, in the autumn of 1870. Mrs Greig, who was in her eighty-fourth year, had learnt the ballad from *her* grandmother when she was a girl. 'Many old people in the parish know the ballad and can repeat a verse or two from it,' wrote Forbes, 'and all agree that it is of great antiquity.' When he asked Mrs Greig how old the ballad was supposed to be when she was young, she replied, 'Oh, just as auld as it is yet.' The old lady had sung it as a girl. It had escaped her memory as the years passed, but in old age it all came back.

A reader from Macduff, signing himself JC, wrote to say he had a copy of the ballad in pamphlet form. He also had an older version of it, printed in Aberdeen. Together, they gave a fascinating account of the 'grisly ghost' that stalked the byways of Fyvie more than a century ago.

Bairnsdale was a small farm between Fyvie and Woodhead. It was there that a widow woman who lived in the house was tormented by the 'grisly' apparition. This is how she described her encounter with the ghost:

I'm the Widow of Bairnsdale
An' I live on the ley,
An' the grisly ghaist comes to my door

I' the mornin' afore day.

He winna gang awa' frae me
For shout nor yet for cry;
He winna gang awa' frae me
I' the mornin' afore day.

He winna gang awa' frae me
For shout nor yet for cry
Till ye take his bones to holy ground
Fra' the hole in whilk they lie.

The widow, who was 'sick an' like to dee' from the ghost's visits to Bairnsdale, sent for her two sons and told them to 'gang seek the hole that he lies in'. To help them they had to find 'eleven buirdly men well armed from head to heel,/ and as many good grey hounds that could bark and bite as weel'.

The earlier edition of the ballad tells how the earth began to shake when the ghost appeared and the 'buirdly men' took to their heels

An' a' the eleven armed men
They ran awa' wi' speed;
An' a' the eleven grey hounds
They ran as they were mad.

Another version of the ballad gives a different account. Here, the eleven men were told to search the woods 'a' roun'' until they came to the spot where the ghost's body had been put down. The dead man had been a forester in the wood and 'was kilt in red war slain' at the foot of a greenwood tree.

And ye maun take eleven gray hounds
Can bark an' bite fu' well,
To warn ye when ye come to the spot
Where his murder'd body fell.

And ye maun take his body awa'
To Saint Mary's blest kirkyard,
And he winna come back to Bairnsdale
Nor mair be seen nor heard.

They gather'd the men to Saint Mary's Kirk,
And the staunch sleuch hounds also,
And a' Ardlogie's wilesome braes
They've driven them to an fro.

They sought him up the Fernie bank
And down the Fernie brae;
But in the den o' Dinnielair
His murdered body lay.

O mark and moonless was the night,
And loud the dogs did bark
When they came to that evil place
Where he was seen when dark.

O loudly bayed the good bloodhounds,
As soon as they came near;
And then the grizly ghost, I trow,
Right awesome did appear.

Ye'll go down and further down,
To the fit o' yon greenwood tree;
And there you'll find my bod laid
Where Warstling murdered me.

I've stood into Saint Mary's Kirk door,
Heard my name cursed thrice,
An' a' for a pair o' dog-skin gloves,
Three ha-pennies was the price

Ye'll bury me among the Christian mools [dead]
As soon as ever you can,
And I'll never come back to Bairnsdale
To fear either women or man.

They've buried him by Saint Mary's Kirk,
Near to Saint Mary's queir,
And he never was seen at Bairnsdale
Man nor women to fear.

In February 1894 the SN&Q editor received a letter from John Fullerton, one of their contributors. He said that he was the man who wrote 'The Ghaist of Bairnsdale' and published it anonymously in 1870. He explained how it came about. In the summer of 1870 he was with some friends when one of them said he had been unable to get hold of an old ballad that featured a wandering ghost. It was suggested that Fullerton should try his hand at bringing back the ghost – and that's what he did. 'Before we left the bents that lovely evening,' wrote Fullerton, 'the ballad was under way, and within a night or two the sixteen stanzas were in black and white' Fullerton piled on the drama in this new edition. His was the most powerful of the three versions:

> Oh, weirdly wild is Dennilair
> When claps o' thunner rend the air,
> An' forked lightning's vivid glare
> Sets hills aflame.

However, in the end peace comes back to Dennilair:

> Weird Dennilair is weird nae mair;
> The ghaist is laid, an' flowries fair
> Bloom ower his grave an' scent the air
> Baith nicht and day.

When I walked down by Dennilair I was thinking of that last ballad. Fullerton's name wasn't on it – the ballad carried a nom de plume Wild Rose, and a brief introduction indicated that it was 'at one time commonly known in the district of Fyvie'. Dennilair, it added, was 'a picturesque ravine which runs directly from the Parsonage, All Saints, Woodhead, to the River Ythan.' It was 'one of the loveliest spots in a district famed for its beautiful scenery'.

4

THE MUCKLE SPATE

The old farmhouse of Affrusk snuggles into the lap of a rocky knoll called the Craig of Affrusk, south of Banchory. It lies near the Water of Feugh, which comes romping down to meet the River Dee. This is the land of the Muckle Spate and there are still farms there whose names recall the fearsome deluge that descended on Deeside in 1829. I went up there, chasing ghosts, looking for farms like Bogindreep, for it was near here that a cadget body [tinker] Johnny Joss, lost 'shaltie, cairtie, creels an' a' at ae unlucky sweep'.

The Shetland pony, a cart, creels, and other goods collected by the cadger, were lifted up by a mountain of water and carried out of sight. I was thinking, too, of other folk who suffered – and of a clucking hen from Ennochie which had been spotted sitting on a kist as it sailed away to goodness knows where. The folk who saw it wondered if it would be carried out to sea and speculated on whether it would rear its brood like hens or water coots. It was last seen near the Burn of Affrusk.

That day, a Friday, a small boy called David Grant stood in the doorway of the Affrusk farmhouse and watched in awe a storm 'the like of which had never been seen since Noah's flood'. He saw how aul' Willie Wilson lost his coo and he heard Meg Mill – Birlin' Meg – cry out that the world had come to at end. Davie was six when the Muckle Spate came raging into his back yard. He never forgot what he saw. Twenty years later he wrote a poem about it. This is how it started:

Tho' I was only but a bairn
In auchteen twenty-nine,
The mem'ry o' the Muckle Spate
Has never left my min'.

That poem, 'The Muckle Spate of Twenty-nine', became a classic and the house at Affrusk in turn became the birthplace of one of Scotland's notable Doric poets. Oddly enough, there were two poets born at Affrusk. Davie was born there in 1823, but eighteen years before that his cousin, Joseph Grant, was born in the same farmhouse. He was also a budding poet and both cousins were to leave their mark on the literature of the North-east, but in different ways.

Davie was one of a family of eight. During the summer he worked with his father as a wood-sawyer and in winter he attended classes at Marischal College. 'I can't help writing verses,' he once said. 'I must write – it is part of my life.' It was said of his writing that he had 'an easy, pleasant swing rarely found outside the old balladmongers'. In the late nineteenth century he wrote his highly successful *Lays and Legends of the North*. One of the poems in it was the 'The Muckle Spate of Twenty-nine'.

The countryside east of the Water of Feugh is thickly wooded, great trees hugging the crofts and farms that were tormented by the Muckle Spate. It is a corner of Deeside that seems to be cut off from the outside world, a place where, if the old tales are to be believed, unspeakable creatures came snarling out of the woods in the dark. David Grant showed little interest in the supernatural, although a witch was known to haunt the district where he lived. But he did write a poem about one: 'a wrinkled hag with a straggling beard and a threatening nose and chin'. The poem was called 'The Witches' Wind', and it was said to be 'a yarn that's Gospel true,' but I doubt if anybody nowadays has even heard of it.

David's cousin, on the other hand, was obsessed by ghosts and ghoulies and things that go bump in the night. In 1828, Joseph published a small volume of legends, miscellaneous poems and songs entitled *Juvenile Lays*. 'The merit of the pieces it contains is very unequal,' wrote William Walker in *The Bards of Bon-Accord*, 'but crude and premature as most of them are, no one can peruse the volume without seeing where the strength of Grant's genius lay'. In other words, Joseph was writing his way into literary fame on the backs of banshees and hobgoblins.

Walker said that Joseph was 'wise in all that pertained in kelpies, mermaids, spunkies, fairies and other more gruesome forms of the supernatural'. He mentioned one of Joseph's poems, 'The Peddler's Ghost', and he quoted from a verse about a local witch with the curious name of 'Eddie M'Tavish'. She was 'the reputed witch of the district' and had 'charms for mischief':

Ken ye auld Eddie o'the ferny howe?
A wrinkled wife o'foursome years an' twa;
Eild's winter cauld, hath clad her palsied pow
Wi' locks as white as wreaths o' drifted snaw.

This is followed by a mind-boggling list of Eddie's 'charms' – 'an owlet's een, a fumert's maw, beak an' sours o' hoodie craw, puff-ball powder steeped in hemlock dew'!

They say wi' charms like that she'll witch a cow!
Can raise the win' an' even (Lord keep's) the deil!

The figure of this 'uncanny wife' seemed to recur years later when Joseph wrote 'The Witch of the Grampians'. He gave her a few more charms:

She could sail the river in a nut-shell sae wee,
When kelpies scraiched at e'en –
And she could fly through the drumlie sky [gloomy}
On the stem o' the rag-weed green.

Mid scroggs an rocks her cottage stood, [shrubs]
On a moor right bleak and bare;
An' on ilka last night o' the auld moon's light
Mony witches an' deils met there.

When I was travelling through this land of witches and bogles I came upon the farm of Gellen. Joseph Grant wrote about 'The Ghost of Gellen', but there were no wraiths floating about when I was there. Gellen was given in *The Place-Names of Aberdeenshire* as the Mill of Gellen (1696) and Meikle Gellen. Locally, it was once known as the Shire o' Gellan, although why it got that grandiose title I never discovered.

Then there was the 'dog o' Gellan', a 'peer brute' called Watch whose sad tale was told in David Grant's poem. During the spate, Watch saw a stick come flying through the air and leapt after it. Both stick and dog ended up in the boiling Feugh. Watch was never seen again. Maybe, like Ennochie's clucking hen, it landed on a passing kist and went sailing out to sea.

The author Nigel Tranter once described Gellen as 'now only a farm but once famous as a "town so-called". Presumably he meant a ferm toun, a farm township, but its fame would have come from the fact that in 1644 there was 'a supernatural conflagration' at Gellen. The historian John Spalding wrote of it as 'a fearful unnatural fire, whilk kindled of itself and burnt the bigging [building] of the town only'.

Old names from the 'The Muckle Spate of Twenty-nine' jump out at you as you make your way through the Feughside woods: Dalsack, the Mill of Cammie, Blackness, the Clinter Mill, Bogindreep, the Mill o' Stra'an.

The Water of Feugh rises high on Mount Battock, near the Angus border, and runs for twenty miles to the Dee. It has been said that the scenery at the bridge is among the finest on Lower Deeside. There was a

The farm of Gellan

'The water raise an' filter't in/At ilka cranny hole'

line of sightseers gaping down into the river when I arrived, waiting for fish to jump, or maybe hoping to see a mini spate burst out.

Watching them, I was thinking of Davit o' the Toll o' Feugh. He was a man who 'like't the drappie weel', and on the night before the spate he and his friends, souter Spriggs and tailor Twist, drank a good deal more than a drappie. When his cronies left, Davit sank beneath a table. Meanwhile, 'aye the rain cam' doon'.

> Abeen the brig, abeen the brae,
> Up to the window sole [sill]
> The water raise an' filter't in
> At ilka cranny hole.
> The water roun' the settle plashed
> An hoor ere brak o'day;
> The tollman wauken't up an' baw'lt –
> Fair play! My boys, fair play!
> I winna drink anither drap!
> My head is like to rive, [burst]

An' gin ye jilp it doon my throat,
Then you and I'll strive.

Davit's wife, ail' Eppie, came down the stairs and when she saw the state of things 'she nearly swoon't'. Eppie tells her man to 'come up the stair, ye senseless gowk, unless ye want to droon'. The curtain is dropped on what happened after that, but neighbours always blamed the spate for thinning Davit's hair.

When I was prowling around the banks of the Feugh I was thinking of the storms and spates that are ravaging the world today, destroying whole cities, claiming thousands of lives. Beside such disasters, the toll on the Feugh seems insignificant – counted, you would think, by the loss of harn sarks. But how would it be if another Muckle Spate came two centuries later, when people are worrying about global warming and all its fearful consequences? Well, maybe we should listen to Birlin' Meg, who told a herd boy to 'rin laddie, rin to Clochnaben, the world's at an end!'

The days have come fan Scriptur' says
The fouks in toons fa be,
Sall leave their hames an' worldly gear,
An' to the mountains flee.
Rin laddie, rin, and dinna stan'
An' stare as ye were wud,
For Gweed forgie's, the sins o' men [forgive us]
Have brocht a second flood.

5

THE WILD SCOTS

Then to Montrose and to Barvye
And so through the Meernes to Cowy as I wene,
Then 11 myles of moor pass to Aberdyne.

When I wrote *Grampian Ways* some twenty-five years ago I included the above lines written by John Hardyng, who was sent to Scotland during the reign of Henry V to obtain deeds that were supposed to confirm the superiority of England. His chronicle was originally intended for Richard, Duke of York, but was not completed in its final form until York's death. Hardyng was one of a host of travellers who came north four or five centuries ago to visit Scotland and to explore 'all the mountanes, drye mosses and wete where the wild Scots do dwel'.

His report took the form of a marathon poem, thirty-two seven-line verses, which were intended to show 'the distaunce and miles of the tounes in Scotland, and ye waye howe to conveigh an armie as well by lande as water into the chiefest partes thereof'.

I remember using the chronicle as a kind of map, marking off the places Hardyng visited, following his route to 'Falkeland' and over 'the highe Oyghylles [Ochills], whiche some mene call montaignes, and some felles', then into Angus and 'the Kerse of Gowry, a plentifull countree of corne ands catell'. He visited 'Fyfe, a countrie freshe and gay', rode to 'S. Andrewes towne' and went north to 'Chatnesse [Caithness]'. He also saw 'the Water of Foorth, wyth hulke and barge, of no smal quantite'.

The chronicle would be a nightmare to most people, but it is a delight to place-name addicts. Hardyng mentions such tongue-twisting names as Camskinelle [Cambuskenneth], Knagorne [Kinghorn], and the foorde of Tips, which turns out to be the lowest ford on the Forth, called the Drip.

He wrote about the water of Tay being 'so navygable for all suche shippes as bee ablee,' about 'Scone abbay, wher alwayes thei crowne their kings maieste', and about the 'mounthes whych some do cal mountaynes in our language'.

He came to 'Dundye' and to new country, the North-east, and this is what he wrote:

Than ryde Northeast all alongest the see,
Ryght from Dunde to Arbroith as I mene,
Than to Montrose, and to Barvye,
And so through the Meernes to Cowy as I wene,
Then xii myles of moore passe to Aberdyne,
Betwyxt Dee and Done a goodly cytee,
A marchant towne and universytee.

Of the whych thirty myles there is,
Of good corne lande, and large extente.
Full of catell and other goodes I wysse,
As to moore lande and heth dothe wele appente, [suit]
From Brichen cytee to the orient,
Where doothe stande upon the see,
A goodly porte and haven for your navy.

Where that the same may easely you mete,
To vitayle your armye, whersoever ye go,
Over all the mountaynes, drye mosses and wete,
Wher the wild Scots do dwel, then passe unto,
That is in Mare and Garioth also, [Gairoch]
In Athill, Rosse, Sutherland, and Chatnesse,
Mureffe, Lemox, and out ysles I gesse. [Moray]

And when ye have that lande hole conquered,
Return agayne unto Strivelyne, [Stonehaven]
And from thence to Glasco homewards,
Twenty and foure myles to S. Mongos shrine,
Wherw your offeryng shall from thence decline,
And pass on forthwarde to Dumbertayne,
A castell stronge and harde for to obteine.

So on it went on. Hardyng visualised a triumphant return from the North. 'From Dumfries to Carlill' he said, they would 'ride xxiii miles of veray redy waye' and would 'wynne the lande on every syde'. He said there would be 'morrow forraies' [future forays] which would 'sore offend' and they would burn 'Jedburgh, Hawike, Melrose and Lader, Codingham Douglasse, and the toune of Dombarre.' He was sure they would 'well quenche the cruell enmitee' south of the Scottish sea – the Firth of Forth.

His chronicle ended with these lines:

Now of this matter I have sayed mine intent,
Like as I could espye and diligently inquire,
Whiche if it may your highnesse well content,
It is the thing that I hartely desire;
And of your grace no more I dose require,
But that your grace will take in good parte,
Not only my peins, but also my true harte.

Hardyng's picture of Scotland was said to be much more favourable than many others. Over the years, I have found myself on the heels of a number of travellers who centuries ago came tramping over 'the mounthes whych some do cal mountaynes'. Men like Jean Froissart, a priest in the time of David II, who 'loved to see dances, jousts and late vigils,' and Richard Franck, a Cambridge man, who toured Scotland in 1656 and complained about the streets in Aberdeen – 'cawses [cobblestones] uncartable, and pavements unpracticable, pointed with rocky stumpy stones and dawb'd all over with dingy dirt'.

Franck was regarded as a good-natured man, a fair one, but it was also said that he made 'unfavourable remarks on the habits and poverty-stricken condition of the Scottish people'. Travelling south from Aberdeen he came to 'a small little harbour which they call Steenhive'. It upset him. 'I take the liberty to call it *stinking hive*,' he said, 'because it's so unsavory; which serves only for pirates and picaroos [rogues].'

Fynes Moryson, another Cambridge man, was introduced to the box bed, which seems to have been invented in Scotland. 'Their bedsteads,' he wrote, 'were like Cubbards in the wall, with doores to be opened and shut at pleasure, so as we climbed up to our beds.' I knew what he meant, for as a boy I often slept in a 'Cubbard' in a croft in Buchan, where my grandfather, old Jock Murdoch, saw out his years. It had two doors, which the old man closed before going to sleep. He at least had blankets, for most travellers had only one sheet, open at the sides and top, but closed at the feet.

They were a motley crew, these early travellers, many with unpronounceable foreign names. Some stayed in Scotland for long periods – Hardyng was three and a half years in the country – others made return visits. In 1861, a book called *Early Travellers in Scotland*, edited by P Hume Brown, carried the chronicles of twenty-four travellers. The first was a memoir, 'The Voyage of Kynge Edwarde', dated 1295. It was written by an unnamed author and was little more than a catalogue of place names, setting down the route taken by the English when they swept through the country. This is what was written about our own North-east corner:

> The Wednesdaie went to Kynge Carden [Kincardine] a faiour manour; the Thursdaie to the mountaigne of Glowberwy [Glenbervie]; the Saturdaie to the cyte of Dabberden [Aberdeen], a faire castell and a good towne upon the see, and taried ther v daies. The Fridaie after wente to Kyntorn [Kintore] maner [manor]; the Saturdaie to Fyuin [Fyvie] Castell; the Sundaie to Banet [Banff] Castell; the Mondaie to Incolan maner; the Tuesdaie in tentis in Lannoy [Enzie] upon the ryver to repenathe maner in the connte of Morenue [Moray]; the Thursdaie to the cite of Deign [Elgin], a good Castell and a good towne.

Another early traveller was the Rev. Thomas Morar, who was minister of St Ann's in Aldersgate, London. I wondered how a cleric came to be wandering about Scotland, but it seems that he was chaplain to a Scottish regiment and went across the Border with them. His account of his travels was said to be 'first in historic interest and value', but it made dull reading.

He was surprised to learn that women went barefoot while their husbands had shoes, and shocked to discover that children also went barefoot. He thought it was 'a piece of cruelty'. He was told there was an ancient law that no males could use shoes till fourteen years of age so that they might be hardened for the wars when their prince needed their service. P Hume Brown couldn't trace any such law, and I couldn't help thinking that some mischievous Scot had been pulling his leg.

Thomas Kirke, author of a book called *A Modern Account of Scotland by an English Gentleman,* published in 1679, seems to have been the victim of another piece of leg pulling. In his book he noted that fowls were 'as scarce here as birds of paradise', although there were plenty of gulls and cormorants. There was, however, one sort of ravenous fowl amongst them that had one webbed foot, one foot suited for land, and a third for water.

Kirke himself had doubts about this three-legged wonder. He thought it might have been the invention of the inhabitants. 'I shall leave it to wiser conjecturs,' he said. More than likely, the Scots were getting their own back on a man who, despite the book title, was certainly no gentleman. He was said to be 'a splenetic and perverse observer' whose pen was dipped in vitriol. He thought that the air was infected with the stinks of the towns and 'the steams of the nasty inhabitants'. He was said to have a distaste for women's bare feet.

'The people are proud, arrogant, vain-glorious, boasters, bloody, barbarous and human butchers,' he declared. 'Couzenage and theft is in perfection among them, and they are perfect English haters, they show their pride in exalting themselves and depressing their neighbours.' He must have realised that he had gone too far, for he tried to stop publication of his book and also attempted to conceal his name. There were quite a number of early travellers who looked upon Scotland with a jaundiced eye, but none were as malicious as the English gentleman.

Jean de Beaugue, a Frenchman who came to Scotland with an armed force in 1548 to help the Scots against the English, had nothing but praise for the country. He thought St Andrews was 'one of the best towns in Scotland,' although its roads were unsafe, and he described Perth as 'a very pretty place'.

He liked 'Monrosts [Montrose], a beautiful town situated in the county of Marne [Mearns],' but here again the roads were unsafe. Dundee was praised as 'one of the finest towns in Scotland,' which might have brought a frown to Aberdeen faces had it not been for de Beaugue's comment on the Granite City. Aberdeen, he declared, was 'a rich and handsome town, inhabited by excellent people'. It had only one fault – it couldn't boast any 'good roadsteads!'

Mr Kirke, the English gentleman, has long since gone, and four and a half centuries later the roads have improved – although some people would say not much. Now, if you were to ask someone, 'Who was Nicander Nucius?' or 'Who was Don Pedro de Ayala?' you would probably get a blank stare in return. Nucius (1549) was a native of Corfu who thought that Scotland was a cold country, and Pedro de Ayala (1498) was an ambassador who said that Scots were handsome, but vain and ostentatious.

There were other pioneers, other names, in the years that followed the 'early birds'. Most are forgotten, but a few linger on – Edward Burt, Daniel Defoe, Thomas Tucker. There was one man whose name still pops up now and again. He was a brash, madcap, penniless London bargeman, who toured Scotland and was entertained by nobles and gentry. He was 'one of those easy souls who are not disposed to haggle with fortune, but take in good part whatever fare she may please to set before them'. His name was John Taylor. Of all the early travellers who visited Scotland, it was said that none was better known than Taylor the Water Poet. You can read about him in the next chapter.

6

THE PENNILESS PILGRIM

Gambling was all the rage in seventeenth-century London. People would put their money on any madcap scheme – according to one report 'whimsical wagers were not uncommon at the time'. Homemade boats were used in some of these 'whimsical' contests. They were mentioned in a rhyme, which noted the 'vulgar wonderment' shown over someone who 'rowed to Flushing from our English shore' using a sculler. A sculler was a single oar moved from side to side over the stern of a boat to propel it. The rhyme went:

> Another did devise a wooden whale
> Which unto Calais did from Dover sail:
> Another with his oars and slender ferry
> From London into Antwerp o'er did ferry:
> Another, maugre fickle fortune's teeth, [in spite of]
> Rowed hence to Scotland and to Leith.

The strangest object of all was a boat made from brown paper with two stockfish – fish like cod or haddock – tied to two canes for oars. It came bobbing down the Thames en route from London to Queenborough, a town in Kent, with two men on board. It was less than half an hour in the water when the paper went to pieces, but the skeleton of the boat was supported by four large bladders on either side. It survived in the water from Saturday evening till Monday morning and reached its destination in safety.

John Taylor, a London waterman, was on board, along with a companion who was said to be 'as feather-brained as himself'. They had sailed into history on a brown-paper boat. Taylor was said to be an expert in the art of self-advertisement, gaining notoriety by a number of eccentric journeys. He was a member of the guild of boatmen that ferried passengers across the River Thames.

In 1618 he set off on a journey that was to give him fame beyond his dreams. His plan was to walk through Scotland on foot. He planned to write a book about it and gave it the title *The Pennylesse Pilgrimage; or, the Moneylesse Perambulation of John Taylor, alias the Kings Magesties Water-Poet, How he travailed on Foot from London to Edenborough in Scotland, Not Carrying any Money To or Fro, Neither Begging, Borrowing, or Asking Meate, Drinke, or Lodging.*

It seemed that Taylor, the self-styled Water Poet, had bitten off more than he could chew. Tramping through the wilds of Scotland with empty pockets was harder and tougher than sailing in a paper bag. But luck was with him. Everywhere he went he was given a warm welcome. He was fed and bedded and even the leading Scottish nobles and gentry gave him a friendly hand. The poet Robert Southey said that Taylor had 'come into the world at the right time, for he had lived in an age when kings and queens condescended to notice him'.

Waterman, traveller, pamphleteer, poet . . . I first heard of him when I was tramping the Grampian hills many years ago. Wherever I went, I was forever treading on the toes of a mysterious character called the Water Poet who had gone riding through the countryside in the seventeenth century. There were strange stories about him. It was said that nobles and archbishops admitted him to their tables, and mayors and corporations received him with civic honours.

Oddly enough, I heard about him again only recently. I had gone to Glenesk to see the grave of Alexander Ross, the schoolmaster-poet, and I learned that John Taylor had been in Glenesk, or Glanask as he called it. He wasn't impressed with it. 'I did go through a countrey called Glanask,' he wrote, 'where passing by the side of a hill, so steepe as the ridge of a house, where the way was rocky and not above a yard broad in some places, so fearfull and horrid it was to look downe into the bottome, for if either horse or man had slipt, he had fallen (without recovery) a good mile downeright; but I thanke God, at night I came to a lodging in the Laird of Eggels land.' The Laird of Eggels was John Linsday of Edzell.

I never found the whereabouts of that 'fearful and horrid' hill where you

Glenesk countryside

could fall a good mile down, but I have a feeling that the Water Poet was exaggerating a little. There was, however, something worse than falling down a hill – there were Irish musketaes. That's what Taylor called the humble midge. He said they were creatures that had six legs and lived like a monster on man's flesh. He believed that they bred in 'sluttish houses' and said that he was living in one. The 'musketae' was much like a louse in England.

Taylor's journey through Scotland started at 'Moffot' (Moffat). He went north to Aberdeen and Elgin and he went to Edinburgh, where he saw Princes Street, 'the fairest and goodliest street that ever mine eyes beheld'. He said he entered Edinburgh 'like Pierce pennilesse, altogether monyles, but I thank God, not friendlesse; for the time of my stay I might borrow (if any man would lend), spend if I could get, begge if I had the impudence, and steal if I durst adventure the price of a hanging'.

Taylor's pledge not to beg or borrow was already beginning to weaken. The farther north he went the more he was tempted to break his promise. People were always giving him money or food or drink. When he stayed at an inn in Berwick a man called James Acmooty, who had befriended him, paid all the charges. He stayed two nights and one day with an 'honourable knight', Sir Robert Anstruther, who not only paid for his horses' meal, but also gave him a letter to a Master George Atkinson, twenty-eight miles away, who 'made me as welcome as if I had been a French Lord'.

So on went our hero, up over Mount Keen, or ' Skene' as he called it, where he saw that weather phenomenon a Scotch mist, which he complained was 'wetting me to the skinne'. 'Up and downe,' he wrote, 'I thinke this hill is six miles, the way so uneven, stony, and full of bogges, quagmires, and long heath, that a dogge with three legs will out-runne a horse with foure, for we were four hours before we could passe it.'

The Water Poet finally came to the 'Brea of Mar'. It was the highlight of his tour. He was a prolific name-dropper and when he wrote about his arrival in Mar he rattled off a long list of 'the truly noble and right honourable Lords' he met: 'John Erskin Earle of Marr, was there, and James Stuart Earle of Murray, as were George Gordon Earle of Engye [Enzie in Banffshire] sonne and heire to the Marquesse of Huntly, and James Erskine Earle of Bughan [Buchan], and John Lord Erskine, sonne and heire to the Earle of Mar, along with their Countesses.' Taylor's 'best assured and approved friend, Sir William Murray Knight, of Abercarny, was present, along with hundreds of others knights, esquires, and their followers.'

Taylor had arrived on the Braes of Mar in time to take part in a deer hunt hosted by the Earl of Mar, one of the great deer hunts that were held annually in August. The statistics involved were staggering – fourteen or fifteen hundred men and horses, five or six hundred tinchels or beaters driving the deer towards the hunters in herds of two, three or four hundred, and a two-hour tally of eighty deer. Taylor summed it up in verse:

Through heather, moss, 'mongst frogs, and bogs, and fogs,
'Mongst craggy cliffs, and thunder-battered hills,
 Hares, hinds, bucks, roes, are chased by men and dogs,
Where two hours hunting four score fat deer kills.

During the hunt, Taylor stayed with the Earl of Mar, living in forest huts built of turf, where pots were boiling and spits were turning, preparing venison, mutton, goats, salmon, pigeons, chickens, hares and other mouth-watering dishes, backed by 'good ale, claret and most potent Aquavitae, all these, and more than these, we had continually in superefluous abundance, caught by falconers, fishers and brought by my Lords tenants to victual our camps'.

Taylor put on his poet's hat and sang the praises of the Earl of Mar's hunting parties in another verse:

If sport like this can on the Mountains be,
Where Phoebus' flames can never melt the snow,
Then let who list delight in vales below
Sky-kissing mountains' pleasures are for me.

He was still holding to his pledge not to beg or borrow money. He had no need to beg, for gifts were showered on him from all around. After the hunt they went to Ruthven in Badenoch where the Earl of Engie gave him a 'most noble welcome for three days'. Other great houses were visited, including the 'sumptuous house' of the Marquess of Huntly, named the Bogg of Goathe. This was the Bog of Gight Castle, now Gordon Castle, and here the entertainment was 'free, bountifull and honourable'.

'There (after two dayes stay), with much entreatie and earnest suite, I gate leave of the Lords to depart towards Edenborough,' wrote Taylor. 'The noble Marquesse, the Earl of Marr, Murray, Engie, Burghan, and the Lord Erskin; all these, I thanke them, gave me gold to defray my charges in my journey.'

Back in Edinburgh, he was given 'a great welcome by many worthy gentlemen, who saw to it that he would want no wine or good cheese'. In Leith, he met the poet Ben Jonson, who gave him a piece of gold of two and twenty shillings to drink his health in England. The gold clinking in his pocket must have worried him, reminding him of his pledge to walk through Scotland without a coin in his pocket, for when he reached the Netherbow port or gate in Edinburgh he 'discharged my pockets of all the money I had as I came pennilesse within the walls of that citie at my first coming thither, so now at my departing from thence I came moneylesse out of it again'.

Penniless or not, the Water Poet held on to the good life. His friend James Acmooty was also going to England and said that if Taylor rode with him neither he nor his horse would want on the way to London. Now, wrote Taylor, 'having no money or meanes for travell, I begin at once to examine my manners and my want; at last my want persuaded my manners to accept of this worthy gentlemans undeserved courtesie'.

So the Penniless Pilgrim came to an end of his journey. He still, however, continued with his tracts and books – and his 'whimsical wagers'. One wager in 1620 involved a journey to Prague, where he is said to have been entertained by the Queen of Bohemia. Many of his works were published by subscription. He would suggest a book he had in mind and then ask for subscribers. He had more than sixteen hundred subscribed to *The Pennylesse Pilgrimage*. No doubt some copies were read by the lairds in their sumptuous houses on the Braes o' Mar.

Taylor wrote an epilogue to the book. It took the form of a poem, a reply to people who suspected that he hadn't adhered to his pledge to walk on foot and not to beg nor borrow during his journey through Scotland. The first verse read:

> Thus did I neither spend, or begge, or aske,
> By any course, direct or indirectly;
> But in each tittle I perform'd my tasks
> According to my bill most circumspectly.
> But as for him that sayes I lye or dote,
> I doe returne, and turne the lye in's throate.

Nobody, as far as we know, 'turned the lie in anybody's throat' about the production of his books. They still poured out. He turned out more than a hundred and fifty publications in his lifetime. Many were collected in a compilation, *All the Workes of John Taylor the Water Poet*, in 1630. John Taylor the Thames Waterman, known as the Water Poet, died in 1654 at the age of seventy-four.

7
BUTLERS, COBS AND COACHERS

He talked of squire-detested poachers,
Of shorthorns, hummels, cobs, and coachers;
Of antlers in his mosses sunk.
Of butlers that were always drunk;
Of controversies about marches,
And of disease among his larches.

I first saw that verse in a series of articles put on the Internet by an antiques company called Old and Sold. It was used as an introduction to a series of 'Digest articles' from very old books. The company had over 17,000 reference articles on a wide variety of subjects, and among them was a book called *Field and Fern*. The author was HH Dixon and the book, published in 1912, was divided into sections for use on the Internet. The first section I saw was called 'Aberdeen to Stonehaven'.

Squire-detested poachers, lairds and their ladies, Chinese pigs that were 'bacon makers', a monument I had climbed twenty years ago, 336 bulls in a Polled Herd Book, farmers who had reclaimed their land from the wastes, and a blood horse called Gouty, I found all these and more in Mr Dixon's book, but what really attracted me were some familiar names. They came leaping out of the past – Captain Barclay of Ury, the Celebrated Pedestrian, who put coaches on the roads in the nineteenth century, and the Cook brothers, who were the backbone of his venture.

There were three Cooks – Charles, John and Alick. Charles became proprietor of the Huntly Arms in Aboyne and Dixon told how he 'took the ribbons [reigns] again' to help Queen Victoria when she was leaving Balmoral to go back to London. 'Although we had put the mare in commission once more,' wrote Dixon, 'we did not wander up Deeside beyond railroads any farther than Aboyne.' The result was that the

Royal baggage was taken by coach and bus to Aboyne to be put on the train.

'It was quite like old times,' wrote Dixon 'seeing them work their four-in-hands with the Royal luggage into the station yard. Alick was there, but attending to the refreshment rooms. The Royal turnspit was the most troublesome parcel to deal with. He wheeled round on a pivot and made his deliveries like lightning if any one tried to touch him; and there was a council of four tall footmen over him for minutes on the platform before he was snared and hoisted with a jerk into the "dog-cage" of the very last carriage.'

The royal turnspit intrigued me. It sounded as if some over zealous servant had been rushing around speedily trying to get the Queen's luggage on to the train. It took me a long time to solve the mystery, but the 'troublesome parcel' turned out to be – a dog!

Turnspit dogs were in use until the late nineteenth century. They were employed to save cooks in large households from turning meat on a spit by hand. The dog was linked to a small wheel connected to the spit so that when it ran the spit turned. In some households two dogs were used in shifts so that neither was overworked. It seemed that Queen Victoria's turnspit travelled with its mistress when she went to Balmoral.

Henry Hall Dixon, to give him his full name, wrote other works in addition to *Field and Fern,* and he also wrote under the pseudonym 'The Druid.' He was called 'The Druid' in his biography, *A Life of Henry Hall Dixon*, written in 1936 by John Bennion Booth. He was well known to farmers and the lairds and knew all about bullocks and black-faced sheep and 'hogging black-faces off the Grampians'. His 'Digest' was packed with information about farmers and their cattle, among them the 'females' at Portlethen – Dinah, Alice, Maude and Beauty. They were 'the principal lady-patronesses of the herd'.

It was to Portlethen that Dixon went when the Queen's turnspit was locked away safely and Charlie Cook's four-in-hands had gone clumping out of the station. He called on the Portlethen farmer R Walker, whose Angus herd – forty cows and heifers – grazed close to the coast. Dixon told a curious story about an ancient sea captain who once erected a steading near Portlethen and called it 'England'. I had never seen or even heard of such a thing, and I wondered if the steading, or its ruin, was still there . . . so that there would be some corner of another foreign field that was forever England.

Another landmark mentioned in the 'Digest' can be seen to the west of

The Boswell Monument

Portlethen – a memorial to John Irvine-Boswell, the laird of Kincausie. It was built by his widow, Margaret, and a granite plaque on the side of it reads, 'He lived to transform the natural barrenness of the estate into luxuriant fertility.' Some two decades ago I climbed Boswell's Monument, going up forty-three winding stone steps which led to a small and perilous platform beneath the crown topping the monument.

Dixon, who called it 'a lofty Greek cross', said it had become a well-known beacon to mariners between Aberdeen and Stonehaven.

Boswell was born in 1785 and died in 1860. He was the youngest ensign in the Coldstream Guards and carried the colours at Talavar, where the French were beaten by British and Spanish forces during the Peninsular War. He often told how he bore a charmed life when two colour-sergeants fell by his side and the flagstick shook in his hand under the shower of bullets. He was regarded as the highest example of an improving proprietor. Only 250 out of 1,800 acres of Kincausie were arable when he took up residence there, but on the 'barren, barren muir' hardly a hundred remained in the original state when he died.

Boswell also had a great love for horses. Ironically, it was a horse that hastened his end. 'A young one ran him against a house and injured his knee-pan,' wrote Dixon, 'and from that time the fine hale form which had seen more than seventy summers began gradually to decline'.

It was his love of horses that took Boswell into another business enterprise – coaching. His house at Bourtree-Bush was where the famous stage coach Defiance did its changes and he often drove it for a stage or two. He was a close friend of Captain Barclay of Ury, the man who put the Defiance on the map. Dixon once told the story of what happened when Boswell and Barclay were talking on board the coach. The pace began to slacken and Davy Troup, the captain's protégé, was heard to say from the back, 'Mr Boswell, Mr Boswell! Ye'll soon be at sax miles an hoor, and that winna dee ava.' Boswell immediately touched up the horses – and the Captain told Davy to 'touch up your lingo'.

Davy, who was one of the earliest coachmen, believed in speaking his mind. 'He kept the interests of the coach most rigidly in view,' wrote Dixon, 'and spared no man if they were jeopardized.' When the captain slackened his pace in the middle of another conversation, Davy exhorted him from behind to 'Gie as mair of your fup [whip] and less of your claiver [idle talk].' Then there was the time when Captain Barclay grazed a cart. 'Fat's the use Captain of takkin' an inch on the ae side fan there's ells on tither,' asked Davy.

Barclay's father was said to be 'a man of will and industry'. He improved 200 acres, reclaimed 200 more from the heather, and planted 1,200 in the space of twenty years. In 1838, at a public dinner in the Glen Ury distillery at Stonehaven, the captain praised his father as a 'heaven-born improver'. 'The phrase,' commented Dixon, 'did not apply to his grandfather, who was quite displeased with his son for carrying a bundle of trees on his back the fifteen miles from Aberdeen and planting them in the Den of Ury.' Like father, like son. Barclays' family were famous for their muscular prowess and pastimes. By the age of twenty Barclay could lift an 18-stone man from the floor to a table with one hand.

In his book, Henry Dixon set down a detailed record of farming life in the North-east a century ago, but he also provided an absorbing insight into the life of the Great Pedestrian. Captain Barclay – his proper name was Robert Barclay Allardyce – earned world renown with his extraordinary walking feats. When he walked a thousand miles in a thousand hours in 1809 his man Cross went at him with a stick to keep him awake. Cross got no thanks – he was 'dreadfully growled at'.

Barclay, in putting the Defiance on the road, brought about a valuable coaching link between Aberdeen and Edinburgh and Glasgow. It was one of the most reliable and efficient stagecoach services in the country. He not only 'managed' the Defiance, but also 'horsed' three stages from Stonehaven to Northwater Bridge. Twelve miles an hour, including stoppages, was the regulation speed, and it kept time so exactly that half the watches in Stonehaven – the scene of a ten-minute breakfast – were kept by it. One guard, Henry Lindsay, took his duties seriously – he would drop off behind the coach, run round it, and jump on again when it was going its best pace.

All the guards had patent timepieces. Their liveries were red coats with yellow vests, white hats and silver-plated 'Defiance-Aberdeen and Edinburgh' buttons. One guard, James Lambert, had a great knack with his whip, and if he passed any pigeons or chickens on the road he would turn round and ask a passenger which he would prefer for lunch, and would then whip it up on to the coach with his thong.

Barclay took pride in his coaches. The first coaches had blue bodies and red wheels and cost £150 each in London. They were beautifully hung and so low that they could not be overset, but the draught was too great and red ones from Wallace of Perth gradually superseded them. In 1838 the coaches were stopped a whole week by snow at the time when a couple of wedding parties were blocked up in a public house near Bervie. The Cooks all but perished one night in riding in with the bags.

The captain was fastidious about his own appearance. It was 'curious', said Dixon, but it 'never concealed the high-bred gentleman of primitive tastes'. He had generally a blue or yellow handkerchief round his neck and a long yellow cashmere waistcoat. In summer he wore a green coat with velvet collar and big yellow buttons, coarse white worsted stockings, as often as not a patch on his knee and moleskins. He had always a little quid of tobacco in his mouth to which he gave one or two rolls before his long, measured speech began.

'He loved to be talked of,' wrote Dixon 'and nothing delighted him so much as when he met a regiment on march during his thousand hours. The officer made them halt and form in double line so as to let him pass through them with all the honours. When he was long past sixty he thought nothing of sending a man on with his dress things and walking the twenty-six miles from Ury to a friend's house and back the next morning'.

He once kept a pack of foxhounds at Allardyce near Bervie, the estate from which he signed himself 'Barclay Allardyce', and hunted Kincardineshire and the Turriff countries, sometimes riding 40 miles from Ury to a meet. Everything he had to do with, said Dixon, was always on a

Memorial stone to Robert Barclay at Ury

The mausoleum at Ury which contains the Barclay family remains

gigantic scale. His cattle must be up to their knees in grass and his wheat wagons – with four or six horses – seemed like an earthquake to the Aberdonians when they rumbled down Marischal Street to the harbour.

At home it was a different Captain Barclay. He was said to be 'quiet and simple'. On New Year's Day he always had friends to dinner and he sat obscured to the chin behind the round of beef which two men brought in on a trencher. The captain gave a speech, a eulogium on those who 'have died since our last anniversary'. Not infrequently he killed one or two before their time, and then he begged their pardon.

His own death was partly brought about by a kick from a pony. For some time he had suffered from slight paralysis. Two days after the pony's assault, when they went to waken him on a May morning in 1854, he was found dead in bed. He lies in the cemetery of Ury about a mile from his old home.

8
NORTH TO SHETLAND

Merrily, merrily goes the bark
On a breeze to the Northward free
So shoots through the morning sky the lark,
Or the swan through the summer sea.
Sir Walter Scott, 'The Lord o the Isles'

I still remember my first trip by sea from Aberdeen to Shetland. I have no happy memories of larks singing in the sky or breezes taking us north. As we crossed the bar and slipped into the bay I could see a member of the crew going round pouring water from a jug on to the tablecloths. I was told that the tablecloths were being soaked so that the crockery wouldn't slide off the tables when the ship was rolling under bad weather. They should have emptied a jug over me for I spent most of that voyage vomiting in a basin in my cabin.

That stormy trip came to mind again when I saw one of the 'Digests' from HH Dixon's books. It told of a voyage to the Shetlands on a ship called the *Vanguard*:

In the eyes of Captain Parrott and his men the sea was of course as still as a duck pond, but when we were outside the bar the prow of the Vanguard began to dip ominously and the ground-swell told its tale in the bay.

Prostrate forms soon peopled all the couches and every inch of available carpet in the cabin. One voice of the night put in its feeble protest against our 'using a head for a football' another groaned piteously when its owner was roused at Wick and told that he was resting over the mailbags on the floor.

Despite stormy seas and rough passages, I became drawn to the distant islands of the Orkneys and Shetlands and their links with the great days of whaling. I heard their stories, of how they hunted the rorqual and the bowhead – the Arveq, the Big One, the Inuit called it – plunging lances into the whale's body and calling it 'tapping the claret bottle', and I heard of how they suffered untold suffering, losing limbs and sometimes their lives. I saw tiny communities with names like Bannok Hole, the Stack of Billy Ageo, and Broonie's Taing – there was once a Norwegian whaling station there – and I learned the shanty songs that the whalers sang in the old days:

> Oh we struck that whale and away she went
> With a flourish in her tail,
> But oh alas we lost one man
> And we did not kill that whale, brave boys,
> And we did not kill that whale.

The 'Old and Sold' Digest articles in Dixon's book filled in the background to those tales, drawing a vivid picture of life in Orkney and Shetland more than a century ago. In those days, the Orcadian was said to be a farmer who had a boat, and the Shetlander was a fisherman who had a croft.

Orkney has always meant one thing to me – whaling! Stromness still has the feel and look of a whaling town. Up on Brinkie's Brae I stood where a 'witch' called Bessie sold favouring winds to gullible sailors, and down in the town I walked on a street where there were no back gardens, only piers and jetties. In the local museum I saw a whale's skull, and I once spotted a whale's tooth in a shop in the Plainstones. It had a whaling ship carved out on it.

When the *Vanguard* was at Wick the town was fast asleep, but flour and meal were being unloaded from the ship. 'A navy of tan or chocolate-sails studded the offing,' Dixon reported. They were fishing boats. 'One by one they came slowly into harbour, some with hardly the tenth of a cran, or only a cod-fish to mock their toil, and others with their richly laded nettresses glistering in the moonlight, like a sheet of molten silver. Four hours more and we are at Kirkwall Bay.'

There was apparently 'quite a jubilee' on the Kirkwall pier on mainland Orkney when they arrived there, where they were unloading, but the *Vanguard* passengers were sobered by 'the thought of thirty-odd leagues between us and Shetland'.

Shetland has been described as a place of wild winds and wild women. There is no doubt about its winds – one writer said it could become 'an inferno of raging gales' – but whether or not the women were as tempestuous as was suggested is another matter. The 'Digest' told how a group of tourists got lost on the road out of Lerwick, ending up among boulders and peat-hags. 'We asked a girl,' said one of the party, 'but she took fright and hurried swiftly down the hill to a cottage, whose women inmates came out and surveyed us with as much zeal as if we were a travelling gorilla'. Maybe they were hiding their wildness, but the tourists had to fall back on their map.

Shetland has nearly a hundred islands, of which about twenty are inhabited. Orkney on the other hand has sixty-seven islands, with twenty-one inhabited. It was to one of the Shetland Isles – bare, bleak Yell – that I made a special journey many years ago. I went there with a boatload of journalists from all over Britain to see an eclipse of the sun. It was said that the best view of the eclipse could be had from this remote corner of Shetland. Some of the country's top newspaper photographers were there to take pictures of it. I was a reporter, covering it for the Aberdeen papers.

We stood gaping at the sun – and glancing now and then at the clouds drifting towards it. Then, at the last critical moment, the clouds swept in and completely hid the sun. Black, impenetrable darkness fell over the countryside – the greatest eclipse of the sun for years had foiled us. There were no pictures to be taken, no stories to be told. But there was a curious ending to it all. When daylight came creeping back again a strange sound was heard – a cock crowing! The unseen cockerel thought that dawn had come. That made a nice addition to the report I sent back to my paper.

The *Vanguard*, pushing its way north, had on board a young English tourist who was always exhorting the passengers to make an effort to come up on deck to see something. '"No," they said, "not to see the last of the water-bulls from the lock of Olginmore."' The seas had been restless but that meant nothing to the English tourist. He wanted them to throw a bottle overboard with a joint statement that they had been shipwrecked and were floating in Northern latitudes and to put their addresses in the bottle, but only one passenger did it 'for peace and quietness'.

Later, he developed a tendency to sit on the bowsprit – a spar projecting from the bow of a vessel – and the sailors warned him that he would become a prey to lobsters. He argued with the mate, who collared him and took him away. He protested that he had sat on the bowsprit between Edinburgh and Aberdeen, adding that he would complain to the steamboat company about the mate's conduct. 'He'll get a gold medal for saving your life,' said the captain. Peace was restored and the evening ended with toddy.

Dixon drew a dreary picture of Shetland as it was more than a century ago. When the *Vanguard* reached Lerwick Bay he wrote, 'We are at the sea-girdled peat moss.' Out on the moors he found the silence disturbing. It would have been terrible even to a seasoned Crusoe, he said. 'There were no bleat, no nicker in the drowsy distance, no cry of the curlew, no "wild birds" gossiping overhead in that peaty, treeless waste. The murmur of a little brook across the road was quite a joyful thing.'

Most tourists, he said, took a pony and a guide and went off after 'thick little trout with red spots', but loch fishing was not their way. They were looking for a Voe. They struck inland to 'a boundless muir'. There was no sign of the lodge they had been told about, but finally they heard voices – 'A house, a bay, and a smack at anchor – the long-desired Voe at last!' There was a kind welcome from a Mr Adey, and plenty of fresh materials for a morning ramble.

Their travels took them to Unst, the most northerly of the Shetland Islands, and consequently the most northerly of the British Isles. They say that if you climb Hermaness, the highest hill in the promontory, there is no land between you and the North Pole, apart from a few scattered rocks. About a quarter of Unst has a skeleton of red sandstone and serpentine, with a thin soil studded with large red stones and knobs of rocks sticking up.

Despite the sandy skeleton and the knobs of rock, Mr Dixon said, 'Still, Unst might be regarded as the heart of Shetland, and a sunny, genial-looking spot it is, when other parts of the country are dismal enough in the northern spring.' The heather and the bog-grasses elsewhere didn't make much milk and the mare ponies sunk so much in condition that they were invariably barren every other year – 'The best ponies come from Unst!' declared HH Dixon.

One of the most striking spectacles to be seen in Shetland in the eighteenth century was a file of forty horse ponies carrying peats across the moors of Unst. It was a sight that was never to be seen again, for the Ashley Act changed all that. This was an act introduced in 1847 by Anthony Ashley Cooper, 7th Earl of Shaftesbury, which allowed pony owners to keep only enough of them for sires.

There was a profitable alternative waiting for them – the collieries. Such a demand for ponies sprang up at the collieries that the Shetlanders couldn't resist the lure of £5 10s at two years old. When the trade was at its height upwards of five hundred were taken annually for the pits, and about two hundred for general use. They were of all ages from two to twelve and for a very good one the pit owners would give dealers as much as

Shetland ponies in their natural habitat

£8 to £10. The year 1857 was a red-letter one and one dealer from near Edinburgh brought over as many as 220 in two weeks and 400 in the course of the season. In 1861 no less than 600 came south by the steamer and about 50 more by sailing ships. The heavy sales nearly drained the Shetlands of ponies.

Shetland ponies were outnumbered in the Durham collieries and the Scots had a lead in Northumberland. Ponies from five to seven years old were preferred but nearly 80 per cent were between two and three. Some ponies hadn't seen the light for fifteen years. The ponies' runs in the pits ranged from 200 to 600 yards. The wear and tear of pony power was said to be fearful, and broken backs and necks and legs pushed up the stable mortality bills.

When Dixon and his party trudged back from the Voe it was 'one of those hopeless afternoons which wets the puir Scotsman to his sark, the Englishman to his skin'. They heard the signal gun boom out its half-hour warning over Bressay. The deck was 'quite a Shetland cattle market and it was Elysium to be once more among the busy band of farmers giving orders about their stock and getting a few last words with the captain'.

The lights of Lerwick were soon far on their lee. The sun was up and bright when they reached Kirkwall and the Shapinsey mail was cleaving her way through the long seaweed tangle.

9

THE KEBBOCK STEEN

The last time I was in Buchan I was looking for a hill with a cheese on it. Not a real cheese, for this was a huge boulder called the Kebbock Steen, which got its name because it was shaped like a whole cheese, or kebbock. The boulder stood near a road where there was a gap in the hills. This was known as the Kebbock Steen Slap, 'slap' being a Scots word for a narrow pass between two hills.

I never found the Kebbock Steen. It had apparently been bulldozed out of the way during roadworks, which was a pity, for you don't find many Kebbock stones lying about the countryside. William Alexander, in his *Place-Names of Aberdeenshire*, produced only one Kebbock, the Kebbock Burn – *Allt na Kebbuck* – at Auchindoir, near Kildrummy. It was simply called the Kebbock, but how a burn came to look like a cheese is a mystery. Alexander himself had doubts about it. He thought the name should really be *Ceapach*, meaning a tilled plot.

But it wasn't only the cheese that attracted me. The Kebbock Steen was near the Gallow Hill, 'the place where the unfortunates who incurred the wrath of the laird of Lonmay were hanged'. Dark and fearful happenings took place on that brooding hill. In 1597 three women were taken to the hill, bound to a stake, and 'brint to the deid' for using charms, witchcraft and sorcery, but whether or not the laird of Lonmay had that on his conscience I never discovered.

Those were the days when ghoulish creatures stalked the byways of Buchan. Water kelpies haunted the fords of swollen streams and

Gallowhill, near Lonmay

will-o'-the-wisps lurked in swamps and bogs:

> Let not dank Will mislead you to the heath,
> Dancing in mirky night o'er fen and lake,
> He glows to draw you downward to your death,
> In his bewitch'd, low, marshy willow brake!

Fairies, elves, guid-neighbours, kelpies and witches haunted the imaginations of our forbears. Witches, old women who could assume the form of any animal, were, according to popular belief, quite common in Buchan at one time. They could 'throw ill' on their neighbours' persons or property, or they could raise the wind to a hurricane and sweep over a whole district.

There were no elves or will-o'-the-wisps to trouble me by the time I got to Lonmay, although I might have been uneasy if I had found myself on top of Gallow Hill after dark. As a lad, I was often taken to Lonmay to visit an uncle who was the local shoemaker – the souter. There wasn't much about it that stayed in my mind. In my innocence I thought that Lonmay was the area immediately around my uncle's shop. There was a post office and a railway station, and trains came puffing up the Buchan line from Strichen; I had no idea that Lonmay was a parish extending north to south for more than eight miles. Nor did I know that it boasted two great mansion houses, and that down by the shore was a huge loch called Strathbeg.

The name Lonmay has appeared in different forms over the years – Lommeth in 1427 and Lummay in 1553. The 'lon' is supposed to mean a bog, which is not surprising in this peat-ridden corner of the North-east. The Castle of Lonmay fascinated me. It is said to have been swallowed up by a great sandstorm that created the Loch of Strathbeg.

Nobody knows exactly where the castle is, or was, or what it looked like. Robert Anderson, who edited the Aberdeen evening paper nearly a century before I took over the editor's chair, wrote a chapter about Buchan's castles in *The Book of Buchan*, but there was no mention of Lonmay.

He thought that these ancient castles 'now in ruins for the most part, and at the best grim, gaunt skeletons, mere shadows of their former greatness, 'possessed an interest that appealed in a very special manner to local historians and archaeologists'''. He dealt mostly with major ruins like Ravenscraig and Inverugie, but threw in a few minor 'skeletons', among them the remains of the Castle of Boddam and a 'fragment' of the old Castle of Slains. But, sadly, no Castle of Lonmay.

There was a piece about the Castle of Fedderate, or what is left of it, for nearly all the best stones were taken away by farmers for building. I knew Fedderate well for it was on Brucklay Estate, where another uncle of mine worked as farm grieve. Anderson said it was another castle without a history, but it did have a history of a kind. In *Buchan, Land of Plenty* I wrote about Mains Crawford, of Fedderate, a man of great strength, who lost his eyesight in a contest with the Devil to see who could lift a huge boulder, known as Mains Crawford's stone. It didn't say who won, but there is no stone at Fedderate now, so either the De'il carried it off or some of those interfering farmers took it away to build a dyke.

But back to the mysterious Castle of Lonmay. The picture that emerged from a muddle of rumour and speculation was that it was one of two castles built by the Comyn Earls of Buchan in the thirteenth century to guard a natural harbour at Old Rattray. This was before the Loch of Strathbeg existed. The other fortress was the Castle of Rattray. There is a curious footnote to this story. A Lonmay minister, the Rev. J Forrest, who was interested in place names, drew up a list of 'places' that had disappeared from the map. One was the Auld Place, which I thought was some old cottar house, but it turned out to be the name given to the residences of old lairds – and the Castle of Lonmay was once known as the Auld Place.

In her *Account of Buchan*, Lady Anne Drummond, Countess of Erroll, drew up a list of the six most remarkable things in Buchan. I called them the Six Wonders of Buchan. Number 5 was 'The multitude of selches [seals] that came in at Strabegge,' but there are no longer selches there and I have, at any rate, always felt that the Loch of Strathbeg itself was the biggest 'wonder' on that shoreline. Here, it seemed as if Nature had snapped its finger and changed this corner of Buchan before anyone knew what was happening. Up till about 1720 the loch was minute, a drop in the ocean compared to the present loch, which, according to Dr Pratt, 'covered about 550 Scotch acres'. There was originally an inlet that allowed small vessels to enter the refuge, but a furious wind blew up and a great sandstorm choked the channel and created an inland loch, which grew over time and has become an important nature reserve. I once sat in a hide on the edge of that glinting water when dawn was coming up and, as if at some hidden signal, hundreds of greylag geese rose, darkening the sky, and flew out of sight. Now, *that* was a wondrous thing!

10

DAME MARIA OGILVY

The track to Bachnagairn climbs up from the long glint of Loch Muick, passes Corrie Chash on the way, avoids a path to bald Broad Cairn, and pushes on to where the South Esk plunges down through a ravine in one great leap. The first time I was there I crossed the river by a rickety old bridge that looked as if it might pitch me into that fearsome gap.

But a new bridge was built. It was made by a group of Dundee hill climbers in memory of an Aberdeen man, Roy Tait, who was killed on Lochnagar in 1981. It took them months to complete and I remember seeing them heaving beams up the hill by tractor, then struggling up the rest of the way with a mountain of material on their backs.

So now the Tait Bridge carries you into a land of myth and magic. Its ancient tracks claw their way over the Mounth, across steep craggy hills and great hanging corries. I once described Bachnagairn as a green gem on the bare neck of the Grampians. It crowns a spider-web of glens below it, among them Jock's Road – even today nobody knows who Jock was – dark Glen Doll, and the long enchanting stretch of Glen Clova.

But not all these old hill passes are 'green and grand'. There is the gloomy Tolmounth Pass, whose windy peat-strewn acres seem to hold an almost palpable threat to walkers. On the first bleak days of January 1959 five Clydeside men set out to cross the Tolmounth, eager to get home, but as they set off the radio crackled out a storm warning to climbers and skiers. They never made it. Their frozen telltale footprints led the searchers to where they had died.

The Tait Bridge

The memorial to Roy Tait

These hills hold more stories than anyone can imagine, some tragic like the Tolmounth disaster, some funny, some fearful, some beyond belief. One of the strangest characters to walk the Angus Glens was a beggar called John Gudefellow. By all accounts he wasn't as good as his name suggested, for he was known as the *notorious* John Gudefellow. He was born without legs and travelled the countryside on his hands and stumps, and sometimes his buttocks. He terrified the country folk, ferociously demanding food and clothes from them. In 1810 he fell ill at Tillyarblet in Navar and died. Despite his reputation, he was given a handsome burial by a local farmer. Digging his grave cost 1/6 and whisky for the mourners came to 13/-. James Bowick of Montrose wrote a poem in his honour:

There's he who slid from Perth to Aberdeen
Upon his hands and buttocks as they say . . .
Who offtimes scared the children from their play:
But now the fearful wight hath passed into the clay.

Country wives may have been afraid of the 'fearful wight', but there were other things to put the fear of death into them in those superstitious days. There were tales of ghosts and ghoulies in all the glens. It was said that Glen Lethnot 'bristled with its tales of the supernatural'. The hillocks on the skyline of the Wirren were even said to be the graves of local suicides. There was a water kelpie that haunted the pool beside Craigendowie and a White Lady who flitted mysteriously among the trees at Leuchat.

I once climbed the Caterthuns, those huge hill-forts which go back over two thousand years. I remember standing there looking across the dark hills and hollows of the Mounth, feeling a sense of awe, and thinking of the Pictish tribesmen who had built that impregnable fortress. They were the first of the Mounth travellers. It wasn't until later that I was told that fairies and a brawny witch had left their mark on the Caterthuns.

I remember, too, climbing up a rough path to Loch Brandy, which lies under the Snub of Clova, where it was said that a witch's curse had foretold that the cliffs there would one day crumble and collapse into the loch. In 1662 a woman called Margaret Adamson was burned as a witch at Milton of Clova and I wondered if she was the one who had thrown that last dreadful curse as they put the torch to her stake. It was obvious that she was no witch but rather someone who had fallen victim to the brutal witch hunts of the time.

There was another witch who left her mark on the countryside and became known as 'the weirdest witch o' wild Loch Brandy'. This was no flesh and blood sorcerer, but a broom-riding hag who was born in the fertile imagination of the Angus poet Dame Dorothea Maria Ogilvy. I first heard her poetry when I was stravaging in the Angus hills. It drew me into a world of soaring eagles and hoody craws, a world where there were 'gorcocks [moor-cocks] chittering on the Sneck o Barnes' and 'yammering yearns' [harping eagles] rising from the cleuchs of Bachnagairn. It showed me 'morning's rosy neb a' tipped wi' gowd' and told me about the 'gleds and whaaps and tods' [birds of prey, curlews and foxes] that scurried about the Angus braes.

Dame Maria was a gentlewoman who wrote gentle poetry for gentle readers. For instance, there was 'The Weary Spinnin O't' which went:

> Sittin spinnin, sittin spinnin
> A' the lea-lang day,
> Hearin the bit burnie rinnin,
> And the bairns at play.

Then, suddenly, she turned away from such delicate verse and reached out to the old Scots tongue, ripping off poems that sent shudders of astonishment and disbelief through the literary world. It was, someone said, as if she had swallowed Jamieson's *Dictionary of the Scottish Language*. Her obsession with extreme Doric took the shape of a tiny book called *Willie Wabster's Wooing and Wedding on the Grampian Mountains*. Published in 1868, it ran to sixty-two pages of closely printed verse. Mind-boggling words like dreddour [dread], skaiths [damages], dirr [unfeeling] and duthe [lasting] poured out from the pages of the book.

Dorothea Maria Ogilvy was born in 1823. She was a member of a notable family – the Ogilvys of Clova and Balnaboth. Her father was Colonel the Hon. Donald Ogilvy, brother of the 9th Earl of Airlie. Most of her early works were in Standard English, but then she changed gear and went roaring into the thorny pastures of the old Scots dialect.

The Willie Wabster poem consisted of some nine hundred rhyming couplets. It took the form of a fireside tale told by an old Grannie, who related what happened to Willie Wabster, a Kirriemuir cattle drover, when he went wandering round Clova's crofts and farms. It became a kind of alcoholic Cook's tour, for Willie liked his refreshment: 'A gill o' whisky, raw, in milk/ Gaed doon his thraaple saft as silk.'

Wabster, jogging through Glen Clova on his pony Mussie, was

entertained at every farm he came to, mixing his drinks on his way – beer, spirits, porter, ginger cordial, port – he downed them all, knocking back three gills of whisky with his dinner at Tarrybuckle. He got cherry brandy at the Manse and a good mouthful from the merry widow at Caddum Farm, who had a soft spot for the drover. This is how Dame Maria described her:

> The widow is nae fag-ma-fuff,
> Nae wudscud, wurlie, woslie wuff,
> Na, an she's never in a wardroom,
> Ye'll never find her glinch and glum,
> She's no farouchie nor furfluthered,
> No tetherfaced, thrawnmou't nor touthcut,
> Nae corkynoddle runk wi' crawties,
> She winna daddle, dunsh, nor dase,
> Nae clobberhoy wi' clorty claes,
> She winna scranch yer corny taes,
> Nor lend a loon a talliwap.

I dug out a copy of *Jamieson's Etymological Dictionary of the Scottish Language* that had lain on my bookshelves for years and plunged into it to find out if that massive volume had really been the source of Dame Maria's poem, or whether she had simply invented some of the words. I found the merry widow of Caddum Farm and had it confirmed that she could have indeed been fag-ma-fuff (which meant a garrulous old woman), and that she wasn't corkynoddle [light-headed] and wouldn't daddle [go slow], or think of giving a loon a talliwap [a blow].

What Dr Jamieson must have thought of his life's work being used in a poem about a drunken drover and a weird witch is anybody's guess. At any rate, I searched the dictionary for the most outlandish words in the poem and they were all from the doctor's list. For instance, there was the description of Mussie, Willie Wabster's steed, as 'A spanking speddart, steve and stark,/ Ay sprack to sprattle wi' her cark.' These lines read like gobbledegook, but they showed that Willie's pony was a nimble beast, a tough old creature tight as a wire, always ready to scramble. Mussie showed her mettle when her master fell into a drunken stupor near Braedownie and the long-suffering 'shelt' was left to take him home.

Here, the story reaches a new peak. The drover is caught up in a nightmare in which a witch from Loch Brandy is chasing him with the intention of marrying him. Not only that, the local minister, the Rev. Ferguson, has joined in the chase with the intention of carrying out the marriage ceremony. They are transported to wild Loch Brandy where a whole coven of witches are holding 'an awful shandy', wrestling in their philabegs [kilts] and sailing the loch in cracked eggs. When Willie's nightmare is at its height, the exhausted Mussie stumbles and lets the drover fall off:

> Puir Willie, when his need was sorest
> Heard the blithe voice o' Banker Forest
> And waukened – lads, haud ye merry,
> Roaring for whisky, rum and sherry
> In the grand market-place o' Kirrie!

Dame Maria made free use of the names of people in her poem, but whether or not any of them objected isn't clear. Banker Forest might have shrugged it off, but the Rev. Ferguson in his manse at Prosen might well have objected. He appears in the poem with the nickname of Forky Ferguson and is portrayed trying to marry Willie Wabster to the witch of Loch Brandy. The minister pops up in the poem on a number of occasions; as the writer Colin Gibson put it, these appearances are 'like a refrain, sometimes angry, sometimes plaintive, sometimes pleading'.

> And ay Will Wabster walloped on,
> And ay the Forky Ferguson
> Cried, 'Haud yer whist, my son! My son!
> And let me get the wedding done'

Then there is a verse with a few words from Jamieson's dictionary:

> For in the river gurgling on
> Will heard the voice of Ferguson!
> And the ramgunshoch, hellish laughter,   [bad-tempered]
> Like brattlen stanes, cam' Brumblen after.

The route which Willie took, chased by his love-sick witch – not forgetting Forky Ferguson – can be followed by using the place names given – names like Craigiemeg, Cormuir and Wester Dalinch. The old grannie who told

Cortarchy churchyard with the Ogilvy family
mausoleum in the church extension

the tale of Willie Wabster and the witch of Loch Brandy put out 1,700 lines of rhyming verse, which must have exhausted her. In the final verse this is what she says:

I'll hap me in my woolen plaid
And creep into my warm box-bed –
Set me a cod aneath my heid, [pillow]
Het water greyneard ben the claes [earthen bottle]
To put some smeddum in my taes. [spirit]
Soond may we sleep till day doth daw
Gude nicht, and joy be with ye a'.

Dame Dorothea Maria Ogilvy gave her heart to the 'green and grand' glens of Clova and Prosen. By all accounts she was a kind, pleasant woman. She wrote some two hundred and fifty poems in all, mostly in Standard English. They included 'Doron', which was written jointly with her brother James Ogilvy in 1865, and Poems and My Thoughts. Her last poem was called 'The Skreigh o' Day', which her Jamieson's dictionary gave as 'a shrill cry, a shriek, an urgent and irresistible call'. It was sent to the local *Kirriemuir Observer* and was described as the 'swan song of one of our sweetest singers.' It began

> I'm an auld, auld carle, and I downa sleep [man] [am unable to]
> A nicht, for I sleep when I may,
> But I'm foremost aye from my bed to creep,
> And I'm up at the skreigh o' day.
>
> Yea, a sorrowful thing it is to grow auld,
> To be weary, and worn, and gray;
> Oh! my limbs they are weak and my bluid is cauld,
> But I'm up at the skreigh o' day.

She recalled her childhood, when her feet were wet with new-mown hay, the peaceful woods and the light awakening the lark. Then old age, when 'ilka joy has tyned [lost] its sense'. In 1985, when she was seventy-two, she said she loved 'this wan warld nae mair' and she wanted kind Death to come and take her – 'come at the skreigh o' day'. She died only a week or two later. She was interred in the mausoleum of the Ogilvy family in Cortachy churchyard.

11
THRUMMY MITTENS

When the cold winter winds come whistling down from the hills I reach for my mittens. They are old mittens and are showing their age. Tiny gaps are popping up in the wool and the 'fingers' are fraying. My wife has repaired them but she obviously thinks they are a lost cause. If I meet people I know I tend to put my hands in my pockets – out of sight.

The trouble is that few people nowadays use the old-fashioned mitten. There are two different kinds, according to *Chambers 21st-Century Dictionary*. The first is a glove with one covering for the thumb and a large covering for the other fingers together. The second is a glove covering the hand and wrist but not the whole length of the fingers.

My mittens are in the second category, the type of fingerless mitten used by cyclists and farmers pulling neeps. There is a song called 'The Mitten Song' which goes:

Thumbs in the thumb place
Fingers all together,
This is the song
We sing in mitten-weather.

Not long ago I made up my mind to put my tattered mittens into the recycling bin, but I changed my mind when I read a poem called 'The Thrummy Mitten'. The word 'mitten' apparently comes from the French *mitaine*. The poem was written a century and a half ago by Alexander

Thrummy mittens

Gordon, an Aberdeen poet who couldn't 'thole' what he called 'foreign gloves'. Born in 1811, Gordon was an eccentric character who was known by the nom de plume the Planter. He trained as a shoemaker and then became a clerk in the Grandholm Works, but was fired when a piece he wrote appeared in a sheet called the *Aberdeen Shaver*, which poured out malicious gossip about local people, mostly in high places. Case after case was brought against the *Shaver* for libel. It closed down, but was back again in 1837and lasted until 1840.

William Walker, in his *Bards of Bon-Accord*, said that the extent of Gordon's literary ambition was to sell his work to the local papers. 'He had no higher ambition than seeing his efforts from time to time in the Poets' Corners of the local newspapers, or of enjoying the boisterous laughter of the village clodpoles as they guffawed over his latest lampoon.' A clodpole was a dull or stupid person.

His actions might have made some people think that there was a touch of the clodpole about the poet. Walker told how Gordon 'indulged in freaks which showed the eccentricity of his character'. He was standing in a shop one Saturday night when a customer entered and asked for change for a one-pound note. 'A pound note!' exclaimed Gordon eagerly. 'Oh, let me see it, it's lang, lang since I saw ane.' The note was handed to him. 'He handled it lovingly, gazed at it longingly, gently rubbed it between his fingers, and with a sigh and a mournful shake of the head, handed the rarity back to its owner.'

The people interested in Gordon's work weren't all clodpoles. One man, a WP Smith, liked Gordon's verse so much that he collected many of his poems. Between 1847 and 1850 he gathered over forty of them. If it hadn't been for this enthusiastic collector, Gordon's name would have fallen into oblivion. Ironically, just before he died Gordon expressed a desire to see all his verses collected, but it was said that 'the careless habits of his best years' made it almost impossible.

After he was fired from Grandholm he left Aberdeen for Dundee and joined the 78th Highlanders, but he later got his discharge by shamming insanity. When he left the barracks he stood outside the gate, slapped his hand on his pocket, laughed at the soldiers behind the gate and said, 'I'm safe noo, there's nae madness in me!'

In 1846 he married and three years later moved to Cluny, where he became tenant of a small croft at Laggan. When his family grew up he shifted to Inverurie, but nothing of any value came from his pen except an Aberdeenshire legend called *The Phantom's Chase*. William Walker believed that Gordon had great talent, but had wasted it. He criticised him for writing and printing 'such twaddle as "The Portstown Ploughing Match"' and for 'descending to the squib and wishy-washy chroniclings of countryside cacklings'. On the other hand, he thought the poet could 'sing with grace the most homely subjects'. And one of the homely subjects was, or course, 'The Thrummy Mittens':

For when the year grows cauld and auld!,
And Boreas snaw and sleet is spittin',
I hap my fingers frae the cauld
Within my thick and thrummy mitten

Or when I gang the neeps to pu',
And snaw wraiths on the tap are sittin',
I wadna ken weel how I do
Without my couthie thrummy mitten.

It wasn't an ordinary mitten that the versifier wrote about. It was a 'thrummy' mitten. The word leapt out from every verse, but I had no idea what it meant. I raked through dictionaries and saw throombs, thrummles and thrumps, but no thrummys. One dictionary gave 'thrum' as the purring of a cat, but then produced the mysterious 'thrummy' – 'a very coarse woollen cloth with rough, tufted surface'.

So the poem went on, and always the 'cauld-proof thrummy mittens', as Gordon called it, hovered in the background waiting to repel the frost and ice. The poem took up with the guidman [good man]:

The guidman when he taks a walk –
His staff into his hand is fittin'
Cried, 'guidwife, rax up to the bank [reach]
And hand me down my thrummy mitten.'

In winter, when I yoke the plough,
My fingers would by frost be bitten –
I find a faithful friend in you,
My cosh and cost thrummy mitten. [snug]

The weeist callant in the house [fellow]
Will rive his claes or lose a button;
He cares na' though they should hang loose,
If he gets on the thrummy mitten

When driftin' snaws choke barn and byre,
And to the stack there's scarcely gettin',
We would na' get a spunk of fire
If he gets on the thrummy mitten.

When round the ingle in a raw,
Wi' supper pack'd till nearly splittin'
We ne'er forgot to dry or thaw
The wet or frozen thrummy mitten

I wondered what Gordon would have thought of that explanation of it all. Perhaps he would have said very little, for in his later years the fire had gone out of him. The man who made the clodpoles laugh had changed with the years. According to Walker, Gordon had become 'a kind, social, genial-hearted man'.

Walker hoped that Gordon's poems would place him more permanently and prominently in the public eye, but he is not well remembered. It may be that he never shook off the clodpole connection. It was said that he appeared to be a 'character' rather than the man of genius that he was. He died on 4 February 1873.

12

PORRIDGE

Back in 1992 I was asked to do an introduction to David Toulmin's *Collected Short Stories*. Toulmin's work, I wrote, was set in the weet and clorty soil of Buchan. It was a vanished land that he wrote about – a land of nicky-tams, fee'd loons, kitchen deems, sharny boots, chaumers and bothy nichts. I should have added brose to the list. 'The Buchan of Toulmin's youth,' I said, 'was often harsh and uncompromising'. Those were the days when the daily diet for a farm servant was brose [oatmeal and boiling water stirred together and seasoned with salt]. On Sunday you got porridge [oatmeal boiled slowly in water and seasoned with salt] instead of brose.

Toulmin wrote about Elsie Wabster, mistress at the Dookit Farm. She wore the breeks and would have won the prize for the most tightfisted housekeeper in Buchan. She fed the farm workers on brose: 'Ye got cabbage brose, kale brose, neep brose, melk [milk] brose and ordinar brose.' Other dishes included 'chappit tatties [mashed potatoes], skirlie [oatmeal and onions], stovies [thick potato stew with onions and minced meat], hairy tatties [mashed potatoes and salt dried fish] and oat bried', and there was another curious dish called 'peel and ate tatties,' which made me wonder if you had to eat them raw? Luxury, said Toulmin, was 'a wee bit o butter about the size of yer thoom-nail'. You could always tell it was Sunday because you got porridge for your breakfast instead of brose. 'Nae sooner was Sunday by than ye was back tae the kale brose again, slubberin like swine.'

I was 'slubberin' brose as a boy when I stayed in my grandfather's croft at Auchleuchries, near Ellon; I supped my oats by a fire stocked up with peat, hissing and crackling, spitting out flames at me. I remember the swey [pivoted rod] in the fireplace and the black pots hanging from it and I can still see the cold flagstone floor and the big box bed built into the wall, with two wooden doors that closed like a trap when my grandfather went to bed.

Bathie was my grandfather's housekeeper. She wasn't a tyrant like Elsie Wabster, but a quiet, kindly woman who went about her work without any fuss. She knew how to handle old Jock Murdoch. Many years after I had stopped going to Auchleuchries I heard that Bathie had married the old man. Today, the croft has gone and a modern house stands in its place.

I never knew Jock's first wife, my grandmother. Her name was Agnes Munro and they were married at Alvah in 1878. I was once told that I had forty-nine cousins on my mother's side. Jock fathered sixteen sons and daughters, but the result of all that was that Agnes died at the age of forty-six. I often wondered how a family of that size coped in a farmhouse, but I was told that the brose bowls were lined up on the kitchen dressers and that that's where they ate it.

In those far-off days there were 'porridge drawers' in crofters' kitchens and they were filled with fresh-cooked porridge. When it was cold the porridge was cut into squares for the crofter to take into the hills to eat. The cook Clarissa Dickson Wright recalled how her grandfather was a doctor in Govan and the people in tenements there kept porridge in their drawers and offered the doctor a slice. If he said yes they would pour boiling water over it and reconstitute it.

Brose or porridge? I have made both and eaten both, and still do, but it was porridge that I was brought up on. It wasn't always a popular meal. Dr Johnson's observation on it was that oats were 'a grain which in England is generally given to horses, but in Scotland appears to support the people'. There were certain rules to be followed by the porridge-eaters. You had to stir it with a spurtle [straight stick] in a clockwise direction using the right hand, for if you used the left hand it evoked the Devil. One expert says you have to keep stirring all the time otherwise you get lumps in it. The crucial ingredient is said to be salt, just a pinch of it. Put it in towards the end of the process so that it doesn't inhibit the swelling of the oats.

In recent years the great porridge era went into decline, pushed into second place by the advent of cereals. Now, however, the spurtles are back

A porridge snack bar

out and porridge is making a comeback. Sales of porridge and oatmeal soared by 81 per cent to £85 million, while the cereal market rose by just 13 per cent over the same five-year period. In 2005 the Brits ate 50,000 tonnes of oats. What's more, market analysts predict that porridge will continue to increase in popularity, giving breakfast cereals a run for their money.

Events suggest that porridge is entering a Golden Age. In 2005 a World Porridge-making Championship was held in Carrbridge, and in 2006 it was repeated in conjunction with Highland Feast, the Highland Food and Drink Festival. The Speyside town prepared itself for an invasion by spurtle-carrying porridge makers from Scotland, England, Sweden, Spain and Israel. The title of World Porridge-making Champion is awarded to the competitor who produces the best traditional porridge using oatmeal, water and salt. They stick to the old ways; no one can sweeten their porridge by chucking in a spoonful of syrup or a sprinkling of raspberries. It would be a kind of sacrilege.

Down in Auld Reekie there is a different scene. On the Meadows people are queuing up to taste the products of Scotland's first Porridge Bar. Here they are offered 'a range of organic flavoured porridge', or as they put it 'a blend of organic porridge oats with flavours ranging from the traditional favourite of brown sugar and double cream to the more adventurous creation of white chocolate and roasted hazelnut'.

No doubt such delicacies as porridge flavoured with whisky or raspberries and cream will become all the rage before long for Anthony Stone is a man who is out to change the Scots' eating habits. This college graduate and two of his friends, Bob Arnott and Sean McNeill, launched Stoats Porridge Bars in 2005. The Porridge Bar is not a thing of beauty. It is a 10-foot stainless-steel trailer and has been described as an oatmeal emporium, but it looks more like an American hot-dog stand. Back in Auchleuchries old Jock Murdoch would have been turning in his grave if he had seen that.

13

HUNTING THE BARONS

When I was making my way through the new Elrick housing scheme near Aberdeen recently, it struck me that I was walking in the footsteps of a baron. I knew there had been a barony in the area, and that 'a well-known citizen' who lived there in the seventeenth century had the title of baron of Elrick and Monycabboc. Later, Monycabboc was changed to Monykebbuck, which meant a cheese. The place-name expert William Alexander wasn't impressed by the explanation. 'The allusion is unexplained,' he declared. James Macdonald, another place-name expert, fared no better with Elrick. 'I cannot offer a single suggestion as to the meaning,' he wrote.

Gilbert Hervie, or Harvey, was the baron. He was a man of principle, for he bucked the Covenanters and was heavily fined by General Middleton for his 'Royal proclivities'. He was a collector for the Kirk Session of St Nicholas Church and, along with a Walter Menzies, was 'Searcher for idle people on the Lord's Day.' The two 'searchers' had special seats provided for them in the church, presumably so that they could spot the empty seats and track down the absentees.

Today, all that is left of Monykebbuck is a farm of that name, while most of Elrick, which was an old estate of the Strachans, and later the Burnetts, has been swallowed up by housing.

Hunting the old barons and baronies, I found some interesting stories. At the Mill of Dess on the North Deeside road you can see a large flat stone with a hole in the centre. It is said to be the only surviving 'Hangin'

THIS GALLOWS STONE WAS ORIGINALLY LOCATED ON THE ADJACENT GALLOWS - HILLOCK WHERE JUSTICE WAS ADMINISTERED BY THE BARONS OF BARONY UNTIL DEPRIVED OF THEIR FEUDAL POWERS IN 1747.

ERECTED BY THE DEESIDE FIELD CLUB IN 1962.
"ADD GLORY TO THE PAST"

The Hanging Stone and plaque

Stane' on Deeside, dating back to the days when barons handed out their own rough justice. It was moved twice because of road widening, but now stands on the *tiremod* [court ground] with a plaque, erected by the Deeside Field Club, telling its story: 'This gallows stone was originally located on the adjacent gallows hillock where justice last was administered by the Barons of Barony until deprived of their feudal powers in 1747.' Passers-by use it as a wayside seat.

Then there was the curious Baron Cairn at Nigg. Back in 1894 a contributor to *Scottish Notes and Queries* wrote about how an old woman had told him that in her childhood this cairn was known as Baron Baxter's Cairn. It was used as a beacon fire at night and as a lookout seawards during the day. He wanted to know how a native of Nigg had come to be called a baron. It was thought that Baxter had been the last of the barons of Torry, which was at one time a burgh of barony.

In the Burgess Roll of Aberdeen there was an entry dated 1454–5 that said that Andrew Chapman, dwelling at Loirston, was employed to make a fire on the Cairn of Loirston (later known as Baron Baxter's Cairn) every night up to the feast of St Martin, and to keep a Watchman during the day 'to warn against the English'.

The Kirkton of Leys was the original name of Banchory and it was as Kirkton that the village became a burgh of barony in 1488. Its charter was granted to Alexander Burnard, 1st Baron of the Barony of Leys, by King James III. The baronies on Deeside were Leys (Banchory), Kincardine o' Neil (1511), Bonty (Charleston of Aboyne) 1676, and Tarland (1683).

When I think of those far-off days I can see the baron of Leys come riding out of the Deeside hills:

> Baron of Leys, it is my style,
> Alexander Burnett they ca me;
> When I'm at hame on bonnie Deeside
> My name is The Rantin' Laddie.

The ballad tells of how the baron had gone to France to 'learn fashion and tongue,' but news came back that he had 'gat a lady wi' bairn'. He gave his lover gold for 'lyng ae nicht' with him and then rode home to his wife. She must have been a forgiving soul for she welcomed him with spice cakes and claret:

> Word has gane to the Lady of Leys

That the laird he had a bairn;
The worst word she said to that was,
I wish I had it in my arms.

Alexander Burnard or Burnett was the first baron of the Barony of Leys in the reign of King James III, but there were a number of Alexander Burnetts and which one, if any, had a wandering eye for the ladies is anybody's guess. The old ballads are often suspect and there was some doubt about the story of the 'Baron o' Leys' because there is nothing about it in the family history of the Burnetts of Leys.

'The Baron of Leys' and 'The Baron of Braikley' are probably the most famous of all the Deeside ballads. The latter is a grim and gory tale in which the Black Colonel comes to the gate of Braickley Castle and calls on its laird, John Gordon, to:

cum doun, cum doun
Are ye sleepin, Baronne, or are ye wakin?
There's sharp swords at your yett will gar your blood spin.

The Black Colonel was John Farquharson, 3rd of Inverey, who got his nickname because of his dark complexion and black hair, although it might well have applied to his character. He was involved in many cattle-lifting incidents in Tullich and Glenmuick, and he was hunted relentlessly by detachments of redcoats. He once made a miraculous escape from a party of dragoons by climbing on horseback the precipitous, rock-bound slopes of the Pass of Ballater.

The bad blood between the two lairds came to a head when John Gordon 'poinded' [impounded] some of Inverey's cattle to settle a debt. The Black Colonel and his men suddenly appeared at Braikley and drove away not only the poinded cattle but also Braikley's own cattle. One version of the ballad has Gordon pursuing them, while another has Inverey at the castle gate and Braikley calling on him to 'gang doun to the lowlands and steal horse and ky'.

Here the ballad splinters further into a number of different versions. It was not uncommon for some of the old songs to get mixed up with each other. In the case of 'The Baron of Braikley' it is said there are four different versions of it, all containing anachronisms and inconsistencies and, according to one source, 'mixing up the events of at least two murders'. On top of that, two different incidents are also said to have been

Braikley chapel tower

mixed up in the ballad: the murder of the old baron of Braikley in 1592 and a cattle-raiding affray in September 1666.

The most popular version has the Black Colonel taunting Braikley to come out of his stronghold:

> Open the yett, Braikley, and let us within,
> Till we on the green turf gar your bluid rin.

The baroness of Braikley was not as understanding as the baroness of Leys with her spiced cakes and claret. She urged her husband to 'Get up, get up, Braikley, and be not afraid,' and when he refused, she announced that she no longer had a husband:

Gin I had a husband, whereas I hae nane,
He woud nae ly i his bed and see his kye taen
There's four-and-twenty milk-whit calves, twal o them ky
In the woods o Glentanner, it's there thei a' ly.

The truth was that 'pretty Peggy' had a lusty eye for the Black Colonel.

This is what one of the ballads says about the slaying of John Gordon:

Oh, come ye by Brackley, and come ye by there,
Was the young widow weepin' and tearin' her hair?
Oh, I come by Brackley, and looked in and oh,
There was mirth, there was laughter but nothin' awa'.

Oh, there sat the lady, as blithe as a bride,
Like a bridegrom bold Inverey sat by her side,
And she feasted him there as she ne'er feasted Lord,
Wi' the blood o'her husband still wet on his sword.

In her bedroom she kept him till morning grew grey,
Then through the woods o' Brackley she showed him the way,
Well you see yon green hill that the sun's shinin' on?
That's the hill of Glentanner – one kiss and be gone.

The bold bad Baron no longer stalks the Deeside hills, but in the shadow of Muckle and Little Inverey there are reminders of those dangerous days: the remains of the Farquharson castle behind a row of cottages; *Creag a' Cheat*, a huge rock formation above the Water of Eye; the Colonel's Cave, from which John Farquharson watched government troops burn his castle to the ground.

Then up in Glen Ey there is the Colonel's Bed, a narrow rocky gorge on the Ey Burn. It has been a tourist attraction for many years, but anyone going down to it has to be careful for it can be slippery and dangerous. The 'bed' is a recess on a rocky ledge. If the Colonel had fallen out of his 'bed' he would have landed in a deep black pool. It was said that he shared his 'bed' from time to time with his mistress, Annie Bhan, who was buried in Inverey churchyard.

Back in the fifteenth and sixteenth centuries, when the Black Colonel was rampaging around Deeside, there were between 1,500 and 2,000 baronies in Scotland, according to figures that appeared in a list of Scottish Feudal Baronies. Only about 400 baronies were identified as existing in 1605, which meant that the vast majority of the baronies listed were 'lost'. The conclusion was that they had been overlooked or forgotten, rather than lost in a legal sense.

The list of feudal baronies is massive, page after page after page, from A to Z, starting with Abbotis-Carse [Stirling] and ending with the curiously named Zester in Perth. Many of the names have old spellings, such as Pitfoddells in Kincardine or Kintoir [Kintore] and Murthill [Murtle]. Birnis [Birness] in Buchan was another one that I spotted, for I had an uncle who farmed there. There is an intriguing hyphenated name, Echt-Forbes, which must have come from the time when William Forbes, a great improver, was proprietor of the estate.

The old baronies had names like Auchinhuffie and Toux and Wranghame. Auchenhuffie is now known as Auchenhove, near Lumphanan. It took its name from *Ach na h-uaimh*, field of the cave or grave. It was said to have a link with the remains of an ancient moated building which was used as a laird's burial place and called the Houff.

There was another gloomy side to poor Auchenhuffie. It was involved in the witch trials of the late sixteenth century when the Lady of Auchenhuffie was drawn into one of the witch's machinations. The so-called witch was a Margaret Ogg and the case against her read like this:

Thow art indyttit as a notorious witche, for the bewitching of vmpuhill Agnes Ross, Lady Auchinhuiff, in Maner folowing, to vit; The said vmpuhill Agnes, having bocht a showder of mutoun fra John Duged at the mylne of Auchinhuiff in the Moneth of Merche, fourscoir fyftene yeris; and the said vmpuhill Agnes having brocht the said schulder to the houss of Beatrix Robbie thy dochter, compartner with thee in all they devilische practises, quhair the said vumpuhill Agnes tareit all that nicht, thow and thy dochter tuk out thrie grippis out of the midst of the said schulder, and causit rost the same upon the morne; quhilk being rosted, and the said vmuhill Agnes eating thereof she instantly contractes a deidlie disease, quhairn she continowit the space of thrie quarteris of a yere, the ane halff of the day burning as iff it had been in a fyrie furnace, and the other halff of the day welting away in a cauld sweyt, quhile she at last departis this lyff. And this thow can nocht deny, for the said vmpuhill Agnes, immediatelie befoir her departure, left her dead.

Toux, pronounced Tooks, was at Old Deer. It was one of a group of names coming from tulach, a small hill, but I never was able to find out what was wrong with Wranghame. There were many more tongue twisters in that long list of baronies, some still around today. For instance, Balquhayne [Balquhain] featured in the list and still does, although all that remains of it is a ruined castle near the Chapel of Garioch.

The Leslies of Balquhain held sway over a large area of the North-east. George Leslie, 1st Baron of Balquhain, acquired a number of baronies from his father in 1340 and consolidated them into one – Balquhain. The castle was burned down in 1526, but Sir William Leslie, 7th Baron of Balquhain, rebuilt it. In 1690 Patrick, Count Leslie, 15th Baron, decided to move to Fetternear House, which had come into the Leslie's possession in 1566. His son stayed on at Balquhain until his father died in 1710.

The Leslies of Balquhain were ambitious and aggressive. One of their breed was Sir Andrew Leslie, who won an unsavoury reputation as the Robber Baron of Balquhain. He had a fortified eyrie on the Mither Tap from which he could glower upon the Garioch till it was safe to come down. He is said to have fathered seventy children, most of them illegitimate, and it was also reported 'in one night he got seven children in sundry places'.

The Castle of Balqhain has survived the passing centuries, but now it is a complete ruin. Despite this, there is still a baron of Balquhain, but he is not in the mould of bygone barons. His name is Dr Nelson Lee Len Ying, whose home is at Traylor Boulevard, Orlando, USA. He is a professor of physics at the University of Florida.

There were other barons on the list with foreign connections. A Charles Henry Francis Mack of Stoneywood appeared as baron of Stoneywood. His address was given as Herzogparkstrasse 2, Munchen, Germany.

So they came from far and wide to join the Scottish feudal barons. In Cromarty there was a baron delighting in the name of John Bartholomew Wakelyn Nightingale of Cromarty, and in Renfrew there was Nicholas Frederic Papanicolaou of Finlaystne Maxwell in the USA. A handful of baronesses graced the list, among them Clare Nancy Russell of Ballindalloch, Baroness of Balindalloch, who is often seen at the castle talking to visiting tourists.

A great fuss arose when the Lord Lyon King of Arms announced that he would no longer recognise barons. Alistair Robertson, a freelance journalist and former colleague of mine, has written at some length about the controversy. The 'nouveau baronage,' as he called them, who were often foreigners of Scots descent, believed that the Lord Lyon's edict devalued their baronies. The 'ancient baronage', on the other hand, had little to lose and much to gain, but old families who owned bundles of baronies, yet disdained the trade, saw the soaring value of baronies as a liability.

The ghosts of the barons of old were probably listening to this unruly row. They would never have allowed it. They would have sent a few of the troublemakers to the Hanging Stane and that would have ended it.

14

LAND OF PLEONASMS

I have been out hunting pleonasms lately. They can be found in all sorts of places, among all sorts of people, and in all sorts of situations – on a dead corpse, for instance, or in an empty hole, among couture fashion, on a dark night, or when you are descending down or being elevated upwards.

I found my first pleonasm when I was writing about Mounthooly in my book *The Road to Maggieknockater.* GM Fraser, city librarian and place-name expert, said there was one street in Aberdeen whose name was 'most difficult to explain'. This was Mounthooly, which had been spelt in different ways since the eighteenth century. Mount Hillie and Mount Hooley were two examples. Fraser dismissed a suggestion that the name was Gaelic, *Monadh Chuile,* 'hill with the corner'.

'A more plausible suggestion,' he said, 'is that the "hoolie" or "hillie" in the name is simply a pleonasm, a repetition of the "Mount", as happens occasionally.' That comment sent me scurrying to the dictionary. It said that a pleonasm was 'an expression in which certain words were redundant', as in a 'false untruth'.

After that, pleonasms were popping up right, left and centre: attach together, affluent rich, completely annihilated, different variation, current incumbent, collaborate together, definite decision, close proximity, continuing on. There is another name for pleonasms – tautologies. The word appears in *Collins English Dictionary,* which gives an example of it: 'Will these supplies be adequate enough?' in place of 'Will these supplies be adequate?' The 'enough' was too much. Tautological expressions were often used in legal documents for clarification of meaning, such as 'will and testament' and 'breaking and entering'.

I ran into more pleonasms when I was carrying out research on the streams that run through or under Aberdeen's streets. John Milne, in his book *Aberdeen*, a series of papers written for the *Aberdeen Journal in* 1911, gave twenty-five burns, some with very peculiar names. For instance, there was the Coffee Burn, which wasn't a place where people stopped for their 'elevenses'. Its water drove a coffee mill.

Then there was the Banstickle Burn, which ran along the east side of the Broad Hill, and the Tile Burn, which passed the site of the old Seaton Brick Works.

The Westburn had a special interest for me, for when I was a lad I often played there, dropping sticks into the water and watching them vanish under the brigs over the burn. I wondered where they went, imagining them bobbing triumphantly into the sea, maybe at the North Pier, where I used to fish for 'sadies' [saithe]. They were called 'shitty sadies' because they came down a sewer.

But the burn that interested me most was the Powcreek Burn. The name had a kind of Wild West ring to it, which is probably why it attracted me, but long years later I was still curious about the name – for other reasons. I discovered that the name Powcreek Burn was a pleonasm. It seems that Powcreek means the wide mouth of a pow, an old name for a burn, especially a slow-running burn, so the name was really Burncreek Burn.

The Powcreek Burn rose in a small spring in the side of West North Street at the mouth of Chronicle Lane. Its water was thought to be good for 'sair een' [sore eyes] and people carried away bottles of it. It wandered away by Park Street and passed under the Thieves Brig on the way from Justice Port to the Gallow Hill.

Its route took it under the bed of the canal and at the Banner Mill in Constitution Street it was joined by a small tributary from the west side of the Broad Hill. The Banner Mill was built in 1830 for spinning cotton yarn, and its site was shown as an island in Gordon's Map of Aberdeen in 1661. The island was a willow plantation and houses shown on the map were wooden sheds for storing willow wands.

The Powcreek Burn joined the Denburn, but was diverted to Footdee to provide water for the fisher population. The Fittie folks' boat-haven was called Pockraw, which means burn row, pouk being a Scots word for a burn or a hole. The burn's route was changed later and it ended up joining the sewer which discharged at Abercromby Jetty.

The name is preserved in Pocra Quay, where today oil ships tug at their moorings. Two centuries ago, whale ships were moored there. It was from Pocra Quay that the first Aberdeen whaler, the *Christian*, set sail for the Arctic in February 1791. There was a boiling house on the quay, which brought complaints from local people about the 'intolerable stench'.

Polmuir Burn is a stream that falls into the pleonasm trap. The word 'poll' also means a burn, which makes the name the Burnmuir Burn. The muir was the heathery ground around a peat moss near Whinmill Road. Even the Powis Burn got caught up in this name game. Powis is a modification of the word poll too.

There were bridges of all shapes and sizes over these burns. John Milne listed over forty in his book, including a Plank Bridge, dated 1523. The old Bow Brig over the Denburn was one of them. It figured largely in the social life of people in the Green, Windmill Brae and Denburn districts, being a meeting place where youngsters played and housewives gossiped. The Aberdeen poets William Cadenhead and William Anderson were brought up in the area, and Cadenhead wrote a poem about it:

> Though we are daddies, we ance were twa laddies,
> An' mony a ploy in our youth we hae seen;
> We could scarce be restricket frae bein' ill-tricket,
> When dwellin' amang the auld folk i' the Green.
> Ye'll min' how, like birdies, we flew wi' our girdies,
> Or played at 'kee-how' or at 'smuggle-the-gig';
> While down Renny's Wynnie we chased the bit queanies,
> Or gambled at buttons or bools at the Brig.

So there it is. There are pleonasm traps wherever you go, so watch out for unexpected surprises and don't allow yourself to fall down.

15

THE WILD WARLOCK

Ilka Mearns and Angus bairn
Thy tales and sangs by heart shall learn,
And chiels shall come frae yont the
Cairn-a-Mounth, right yousty,
If Ross will be so kind as share in
Their pint at Droustie.

James Beattie

It is more than twenty-five years since I first went over the Cairn o' Mount and down to Glenesk, making for an old graveyard on the banks of Loch Lee. This was where I found a ruined church said to have been dedicated to St Drothan, a disciple of Columba and co-founder of the Abbey of Deer in Aberdeenshire.

There are only a few old gravestones in the old kirkyard – some have been buried in the ground – and I found the one I was looking for. The old weather-beaten stone told me that it had been 'Erected to the memory of Alexander Ross, AM, schoolmaster of Loch Lee. Born April 1699 died May 1784.' Born on Deeside, he became a schoolmaster and author of *Helenore*, a pastoral tale that made him famous.

I was one of the latter-day chiels who had come over the Cairn o' Mounth, but I was two centuries too late to have a pint with Ross at Droustie's, which was what they called the local ale-house. But I fell in love with this so-called 'glen of glens' and I was fascinated by the story of the dominie-poet who was called a 'wild warlock' by Robert Burns.

So, as the years rolled in on me, I decided to go back to Glenesk to find out if it had changed, to learn if the folk were still 'yousty' [voluble and noisy], to marvel at the great hills around me and to look along the glinting waters of Loch Lee. In those earlier years I had come down to the loch by the old 'ways', past ruined settlements and crumbling sheilings, on land

Memorial to Alexander Ross

where cattle had their summer grazing. Ross wrote about them:

On skelfs a' round the wa's the cogs were set, [shelves] [pail or bowl]
Ready to ream, an' for the cheese be het [bubble over]
A hake was frae the rigging hinging fu' [hook]
Of quarter kebbucks, rightly made an' new. [cheese]
Behind the door a calour heather bed, [fresh]
Flat o' the floor, of stones an' fail was made. [turf]

I was following a route taken by the only man to cross the Mounth in his bare feet, wearing nothing but a nightshirt. Robert Dinnie, father of the famous Donald Dinnie, wrote about him in his *Account of the Parish of Birse*. His name was Duncan Grant. He fought with Prince Charles at Culloden and was hunted by Redcoats in the Forest of Birse. When they knocked on the door of his house he bolted from under their noses 'a man without shoes on his feet, or a rag on his body, excepting the shirt, and that of no very great dimensions'.

He hotfooted it across the Grampians, forded the Tarf at Shanfur, slipped past the bailies and got away. They should have put up a monument to this bold Jacobite, showing him in his nightshirt of course, and they could have placed it by the Maule Monument on top of Rowan Hill, which was also a bit of a curiosity. Erected by Fox Maule, Earl of Dalhousie in 1866, it said that it was 'in memory of seven members of the family already dead – and of himself and two others when it shall please God to call them hence'.

I began my latest visit to Glenesk at Gannochy Bridge, where the North Esk leaves the glen with a flourish, passing through a gorge of old red sandstone where larch trees droop over great ravines and dark pools lie still and quiet below the narrow path along the riverbank. Here, there are two well-known beauty spots intriguingly called the Loup of Esk and the Rock of Solitude. It was from this lovely corner that I set out to renew my acquaintance with the 'glen of glens', starting not far from a quaint cottage where I had stayed many years ago – and been chased by the farmer for tramping on his neeps.

There are sixteen miles between Gannochy Bridge and the end of the road. It is beautiful country, an artist's dream, but I was to find that some things had changed. Glenesk Folk Museum, which was founded by Greta Michie and must have drawn hundreds of visitors to the glen, was no longer there. The building itself – the Retreat – had been given a face-lift, and was now simply a tearoom. The museum, a treasure house of Glenesk history, had gone. No more tinker's lanterns or old fiddles, no picture of Diddlin' Davy, the last occupant of the Mill of Aucheronie, no more Muckle Wheel for spinning; the exhibits had mysteriously vanished. I was told that the museum would be restored later, but I think they should have sorted out the museum first and tarted up the tearoom later.

There were changes, too, at Tarfside. This little community – locals still call it a village – is on the road to Loch Lee. There had been a clutter of houses, a post office, a shop and a toilet, but it was a bare, deserted place

Saddle Skedaddle

when I returned. No more post office, no more shop – the shop used to be a house called Elm Cottage. The toilet was still there and outside it was a sign pointing out a tap that could be used by travellers. They were warned, however, that it must only be used for 'modest' purposes.

We left Tarfside and pushed up the glen, stopping for a picnic lunch. Near us was a big transit coach with a huge trailer that could carry eighteen bicycles. On a bench outside it was a lone figure preparing a meal for the people riding those bikes. They were members of the oddly named Saddle Skedaddle, an organisation that runs cycling tours all over the world. In this case they were doing a cross-country run from Glenelg to Montrose.

There were ten bikers and three guides, and the man outside the coach making lunch for them was Tony Stoddart, a fireman, who was an ardent hill man and had done all the Munros. The leading guide was Steve Woods. The first of the bikers swept round the corner when we were setting off again. It struck me as I watched them that a different breed of riders had come clattering down the glen a long, long time ago. They were the dreaded cateran, Highland marauders.

The sturdy ruin of Invermark Castle stands at the head of the glen, near Loch Lee. It was built as an outpost to Edzell Castle in a bid to halt the

Invermark Castle

Highland raiders who came over the Mounth to plunder the fat cattle in the Angus glens. Glen Esk was often harried and burned by the cateran. An old ballad in 1692 told how more than three hundred Highlanders descended on the glens. Sir David Lindsay of Glenesk was badly wounded in the affray.

Invermark Castle belongs to two periods. The first three storeys were built in the early sixteenth century. The upper storeys and two-storey angle-turret were added a century later, when the cateran menace was at its worst. One raid carried off almost half the cattle and sheep in the glen. Five Glenesk men were killed in a bid to recover their stock and a dozen more were taken prisoner and released after a hefty ransom had been paid.

'In Lochlie was the great and strong castle of Innermark, upon the water of Northesk,' read a report in 1684. 'It is very well peopled and upon any incursions of the Highland Katranes, for so those Highland robbers are called, the Laird can, upon very short advertisement, raise a good number of weill armed prettie men, who seldom suffer any prey to goe out of their bounds unrecovered.'

In 1641, David Lindsay of Edzell complained on behalf of himself and his tenants about the depredations caused by 'great nomberes of brokine Hielandmen carieing away great quantities of horss, nolt [cattle], sheepe and other plenishing fra him and his saidis tennentis'. The cateran had little concern for the grief they imposed on their victims, as seen from a report of a plea to the Presbytery by a George Thom, 'somtym reader of the kirk of Lochlie'. In May 1649, he begged the Presbytery for help for his young children 'in this tyme of death'. He had been robbed of his goods and furnishings by Highlanders.

The cateran and the 'prettie men' have slunk away into the history books and today it is hard to comprehend that such a lovely glen was ravaged by these Highland raiders. There is a more peaceful symbol on the Loch Lee road – the fourth St Drostan's Episcopal Church, built in 1879. Nigel Tranter wrote that it was a fine building, which it certainly is, but added that it 'looked a little forlorn these days'. It was made even more forlorn by 'a rather pathetic notice' pointing out that the congregation now numbered about a dozen. That was in 1972.

St Drostan's was well known as Droustie's, although an old publication, the *Scottish Guardian,* called it Drusty. It mentioned Drusty Hill, Drusty's Well and an inn named after the saint, 'which has now disappeared'. There were other Drousties with a different spelling: Droustie's Meadow, whose location is uncertain, and a Droustie Farm dating back to 1716 and 1758. There is little doubt that the inn was the one mentioned in the verse written by Professor James Beattie.

I was thinking of Droustie's when I went down the hill to the loch. Nobody seemed to be clear on where the alehouse had been, and the nearest anyone got to it was William Walker, who wrote in his *Bards of Bon-Accord* that it was 'a busy, and to the weary traveller between Glenesk and Deeside, a welcome alehouse, which occupied the supposed site of St Drostan's cell'.

The last house on the road to Loch Lee is Gardener's Cottage, where Alexander Ross, the schoolmaster and poet, lived. The schoolhouse was a small building close to the churchyard. It contained two 12-foot square apartments and the Wild Warlock and his family occupied the room to the west. His stipend was about £20 a year. Here, Ross lived and taught for more than fifty years.

The old trails spin away in every direction, into wilderness country with names recalling people and places that were well known to Ross: the Witter (a witter is a stone), Cairn Lick, Horse Holm, the off-putting Mudloch Cott on the Tarfside road, or Tampie and Mudlee Bracks overlooking the Fungle Road. Tracks like the Firmounth and Fungle were the main crossings from Deeside to Tarfside. I remember coming upon an old granite memorial erected by the eccentric laird of Glentanner that read: 'Fir Munth. Ancient PASS over the Grampians.'

These 'ways' and paths were the threads that made up the tapestry of the Mounth, that tortuous landscape sprawling from Angus and the Mearns to Deeside. There was a steady coming and going over the Mounth. Some who went south to the Angus Glens decided, like Alexander Ross, to stay there; others, like John Cameron of Crathie, were as well known on one side of the Grampians as they were on the other.

Deeside was noted for its fiddlers in the early nineteenth century and Cameron was one of them. For more than forty years he made a winter trek over the Mounth to entertain the folk of Glenesk. Alexander Ross was also a fiddler and it was from Cameron that he learned about an old Deeside custom. When any member of a family died a musician was sent for, and before the internment the whole family except the children took part in a kind of dancing. The musician played slow, plaintive music on the violin or bagpipes and the nearest friends of the deceased took to the floor

Loch Lee

for the first dance, 'expressing their grief as well as by their tears'. It was called 'moving to music'.

Ross himself regularly went over the hills on foot until he was seventy. When he was eighty he still made an annual visit to his eldest daughter, who lived with her husband and family near Pannanich Wells at Ballater. He walked twenty miles a day and arrived on Deeside with no sign of fatigue. He died in his eighty-sixth year and he had already written what should have been his own epitaph:

Hence lang, perhaps, lang hence may quoted be
My hamely proverbs lined wi' blythsome glee;
Some readers then may say. 'Fair fa'ye, Ross,' [good befall ye]
When, aiblins, I'll be lang, lang dead and gane [perhaps]
An' few remember there was sik a ane.

Two centuries have passed since the sound of Ross's fiddle drifted over Loch Lee and the Wild Warlock is 'lang, lang dead and gane'. As he wrote prophetically in his poem, there are only a few who would remember who he was – or know that there ever had been 'sik a ane'.

16
THE GLEN OF HORSES

The Glen of Horses lies to the west of Huntly, where the Markie Water joins the River Deveron. Its proper name is Glenmarkie, which comes from the Gaelic *marc*, 'a horse'. It is said that the name 'glen of horses' originated in an old custom in which, during the summer, horses were taken to a glen or a hill with common pasturage.

James Macdonald, author of *Place Names in Strathbogie,* met a farmer who told him that in his youth he had seen sixty horses grazing on a hill to the west of Aswanley, south-west of Huntly. The same practice prevailed in the Cabrach. The Cabrach was said to be a royal forest at one time and tradition had it that it was reserved for grazing royal horses. The host in the Richmond Hotel at Ardwell in the Lower Cabrach said his grandfather had put out his horses on common pasturage on the Blackwater and one of them wandered into a bog. It sank until it disappeared.

Macdonald said the story was useful in illustrating an old custom, and it showed how place names could originate in casual circumstances. For long after that the place was called 'Watt's stable'. It is unlikely that 'Watt's stable' was the only piece of boggy land that claimed an unsuspecting cow or horse, for the Cabrach had more than its share of swampland. There were a number of farms with boggy names, although some tried to hide it. The farm of Bogferge, which took its name from Bog-feurach, 'the grassy bog', became the more acceptable Heatheryfield.

John Watt, the innkeeper who gave his name to 'Watt's stable', also ran a farm. His father, who died in 1912 at the age of eighty-five, ran the farm

The Grouse Inn, formerly the Richmond Hotel

and had taken over the inn in 1876. The Richmond Hotel is known today by its original name, the Grouse Inn, but in the old days locals called it the Airdwell. There were two Ardwells, Upper and Nether. In the early years of the seventeenth century there were thirteen dwellings at Nether Ardwell, but a century later there were only two farmhouses, one of which was also the inn.

The fishing rights for the Deveron and Black Water were granted by the duke of Richmond and Gordon, and before a shooting lodge was built in the Upper Cabrach the duke's tenants or guests resided at the inn.

The Taylor family held sway in this corner of the Cabrach for many years. The Milltown of Lesmurdie belonged to James Taylor, whose forbears had lived there since before Culloden. It was one of the Cabrach 'touns', with several houses occupied by the farmer, the miller and the joiner, and in a corner of the steading there was a building used as a school. If you had gone down the left bank of the Deveron from Milltown you would have come on four farms within easy reach of each other. They were the Tombain [the white knoll], Tombally [the spotted knoll] and farther down the river the Mains of Lesmurdie and Boghead.

At one time during the nineteenth century, the farmer at Boghead was

John Taylor, better known as 'Boggy'. It was said of Boggy that he might well have claimed to be the first historian of the Cabrach. This was despite the fact that he had attended school for only six weeks. Most of what he knew was self-acquired. Nevertheless, he had a thirst for knowledge and he had gathered together a remarkable collection of old diaries and newspaper cuttings that was to become the basis for a book on the Cabrach.

This collection ended up in the hands of Boggy's nephew, James Taylor, who shared his uncle's interest in the Cabrach's history. He decided to expand it, and work began on what everybody called 'The Book'. The research meant visits to libraries in Aberdeen and Edinburgh, and to such places as the Scottish Register House and the British Museum Reading Room. It was edited by Janet Anderson, who played a major role in its production. In August 1914 the Cabrach history was put aside and the manuscripts remained untouched until the war ended in 1918. Sadly, James Taylor never saw his book in print – he died in September 1918.

It was finally published in 1920 by the *Banffshire Journal* and they called it *Cabrach Feerings* – a feering was the first guiding furrow ploughed on the land. However, it could be said that the first furrow in the Cabrach story was *partly* ploughed in 1891 when James Macdonald's *Place Names in Strathbogie* was published. It carried a chapter on the Cabrach, but it dealt with the whole of Strathbogie, not just one area. Macdonald's wider and more scholarly work was indispensable as a place-name guide, but Boggy's treasure chest, that jumbled collection of old diaries and newspaper cuttings, went to the heart of the Cabrach.

It was *Feerings* that brought me back to the Cabrach. It led me to people and places that had long been forgotten. It took me over the hills of Blackwater, where 'the hospitable smell of peat fires rose to greet us,' reminding me of the days when I cut peat on an uncle's peat moss in Buchan. The Glenfiddich Distillery got its supply of fuel from a moss on the Garbet hill, 'so the Cabrach,' it said, 'deserves some of the credit for the fineness of the whisky.'

Feerings led me to Bridgend, 'the nearest approach to a village the Cabrach possesses,' which is backed by the hill of Tomnavoulin [locals pronounced it Tam-a-ooin]. 'At Bridgend is "The" shop,' reported *Feerings*, 'with the Post and Telegraph Office, the Blacksmith's and five other occupied houses. There is another small shop at Crofthead. Not so long ago, indeed within the last thirty or forty years, there were no fewer than eight tradesmen at Bridgend, all of whom found plenty of work: two shoemakers, a tailor, a dressmaker, a blacksmith, a merchant, a weaver and a joiner, but now that people find it so much easier to visit a town and have acquired a taste for town products, these country workers have sadly diminished in numbers.' Today, that once-lively community is no longer 'the nearest approach to a village'.

Coming down through the Cabrach from Dufftown you pass through the Glacks of the Balloch. I have travelled that pass many times, but I never knew that about the middle of the pass there was a site where there had once been a cairn. When I read about it in *Feerings* I thought I was back in Meggie Stott's land, where there was a Witch's Cairn, but this was a different kind of spooky affair.

It was said that a bull's hide full of gold was hidden below the cairn, watched over by the fairies. No one dared to open the cairn until one man went secretly at night and dug a hole there. Ghostly figures flitted around him and ghostly voices sounded in his ears. The hole got deeper and deeper until the stones he had thrown out came flying back at him. Frightened, he decided to wait for daylight and when dawn came he saw to his amazement that the cairn was still intact, with no sign of his digging. He hastily gave up his search.

James Taylor mentioned several mounds that could be seen just before entering the Glacks. They are known as Jean's Hillocks and are said to have been named in memory of a Jean Gordon of Lesmoir whose story was a tragic one. Jean squandered her estate, was reduced to beggary and died at that spot of hunger and fatigue. A ballad of the time told what happened to her, but *Feerings* could only find the last two lines: 'She drank her lan' and sold her shoon,/ And died at Allawakin.' The Gordons of Lesmoir figured in most of the stirring events of their time. James Macdonald wrote about them at some length in his *Place Names of Strathbogie,* but there was no mention of the ill-fated Jean Gordon or the ballad. I was never able to dig up any more information about her or how she died at the curiously named Allawakin.

There was another mention of Allawakin in a passage in which the writer James Macdonald describes what he saw from the bridge at the entrance to Glenfiddich shooting lodge:

In front of us now lies a wild and picturesque region. On the farther side of the river rises the steep and rugged hill of Bemain, along the side of which our road winds its way steadily upwards till lost from view between the hills. On our right, as we follow it, is first the burn of Allawakin, rushing down beside it, then a wide stretch of moor, with hill upon hill beyond, covered with heather . . . on the brow of the nearest hill a dark fir plantation, just below which may be traced the site of the farm buildings of the Brackery, the ground near showing signs of having been cultivated, but long since become part of the deer forest. Frequently, especially in bad weather, when they come down from the highest parts of the forest large herds of deer may be seen, and if it is the traveller's fortune to come this way on a dark night of autumn he may be thrilled by hearing the roar and stamp of the stags as they send forth their challenge to battle.

If they had come down another way they might have heard the roar and stamp of a different animal – the Wormie Dragon. Its tale was told in another *Feerings* piece about the Glacks of Balloch, and James Macdonald also wrote about it in his *Place Names of Strathbogie*. He mentioned the Wormy Hillock and said it was the grave-mound of a dragon which had once infested the neighbourhood and was slain at this spot by some unknown Sir George. He ended by apologising for 'spoiling an interesting legend'.

Feerings, on the other hand, came down to earth and said it was the popular name of the Old Caledonian Road, the highway from Forres by Auchindoun and the Cabrach to the Mearns. It could be traced through the Glacks along the base of the Muckle Balloch, crossing to the Garbet Hill, and then over the Kelman Hill to Boghead. Boggy probably had some information about it in his collection, for the *real* story was also given. This was that two huge 'worms' had appeared in the north and journeyed to meet each other in combat. One started from Bennachie, the other from near the Balloch Hill. The legend didn't say which dragon won the battle, but it described how one of them threw up a number of mounds – Jean's Hillocks!

So there you are. Were the mounds a memorial to Jean Gordon of Lesmoir or the work of a monster worm? Nothing is ever certain in the Cabrach, not even the weather. There is a chapter in the book *Feerings* which recognises the fact that people talk about 'a place they ca' the cauld, cauld Cabrach'. It doesn't help when there is a bit in the book about a section of the Glacks of Balloch where 'on the calmest day a breeze is felt and on a day of wind the gale rushes through the pass as through a funnel and seems to beat back the intruder'.

But the *Cabrach Feerings* takes a swipe at the weather critics in a chapter on 'Weather and Crops'. There was plenty of sunshine all the year round, it said, no fog, warm days in summer, and bright frosty ones in winter. But it admits that there had been 'good grounds for the popular notion' and quotes the year 1836, the year in which the river froze so badly that horses crossed on the ice. During February the drifting was so great that the mails from Aberdeen were brought through only with the greatest difficulty. A party of three carried them four or five miles and were then relieved by another party who carried them the next four or five miles, and so on until they reached their destination.

The year 1839 wasn't much better. A man called Charles Stewart of Haddoch perished in the hills, and a funeral party from Rhynie going to Wallakirk across the hills were compelled to lift and pull the coffin through enormous drifts. Just to complete that year there was a 'remarkable spate' in which the river rose to within six inches of the flood mark of 1829. A number of bridges were swept away by the Deveron.

Well, I suppose the appeal of the Cabrachs depends on how you look on life. When I wrote *The Royal Glens* some years ago I commented that in this wild land it was best to think of the King of the Cabrach. He wasn't a real King: he had a sheltie and a fozelin' tyke [a wheezing old dog] at his side and he featured in Mary Symon's poem 'The Hedonist'. 'I'm a King,' he said, 'I can dae as I leike, an' I'm giein' fowk their fun.' He wanted his epitaph to read, 'He garts a' laugh.' It is pretty certain that the King of the Cabrach laughed his way through all the floods and snow drifts that nature threw at him.

17

KINKERS

This passes from Fittercairne in the Mearns to Kincardyne of Neill on Dee, in Mar, and conteins aucht myles in mounth.

View of the Diocese

They called it Kinkers. In the days when the Cairn-a-Mounth was an important cross-country road and one of the great passes over the Grampians, Kincardine O'Neil was an important centre for the north of Scotland. It was there that the ancient road crossed the Dee, a vital link between Strathmore and Moray. It was known as the North and South Road.

History hugs every corner of this Deeside village. Macbeth came this way to Lumphanan in the middle of the eleventh century, and Edward I of England camped here overnight in 1296 with an army of 30,000 men and 5,000 mail-clad knights. An old rhyme tells how he left the locals with nothing to eat:

O' followers he had a flock,
Left neither capon, hen nor cock,
Na, nor butter, bread nor cheese.
Else my informant tells me lees,
An' worse o' a' I'm woe to tell,
They left them neither meat nor ale.

Edward again stopped at Kincardine O'Neil eight years later but there are no reports that he robbed them of their meat or ale. At any rate, it was Edward's last visit to Deeside.

When I had a caravan at Tarland some years ago I occasionally went down to the church at Coull, where a relative of my wife was buried. I was always fascinated by the ruins of Coull Castle, scattered about in a field bordering the kirkyard. Not much of it was left. In his book, *The Old Deeside Road,* published in 1921, George Fraser, Aberdeen's librarian, said it was strange that in his generation nothing had been seen of Coull Castle.

It was almost as if it had been swept off the face of the earth, and yet, as Fraser said, this was the home of a remarkable family whose proceedings at Kincardine O'Neil gave the place much of the historical distinction. The Durwards were the most powerful people in the region next to the earl of Mar. They were generous benefactors and it was Durward foresight and skill that put little Kincardine O'Neil on the map. In the thirteenth century Alan Durward built a chapel and hospice for travellers going and coming over the Cairn-a-Mounth. The following century, his father, Thomas the Durward, built a bridge over the Dee for Mounth travellers.

When I was finding my way through the misty years of the 'remarkable' Durwards and their vanished castle it struck me that I was back amongst the barons and baronesses. Old records threw up names and titles like 'baronia de Neill' (the area dominated by Alan Durward from Coull), and Thanagium de Oneill [a person of rank]. Neil, Neale and Oneill indicated an ancient thanage.

The barony of Kincardine O'Neil included part of Lumphanan and it was held by Alan Durward. The last of the Durwards connected with the barony was a female, Anna Durward. There is not much to show how the womenfolk fared in those far-off days, but at least one baroness made sure that they behaved themselves. This was Isobell Duff, Baroness of O'Neil in 1388, who gave orders for the erection of a cock-stool and a ducking-pool. This was done to punish women who had done wrong:

> For scolds an' limmers, an' sic cattle
> Wha deal in fibs an' tittle-tattle.

I struggled free from all this confusion of titles and tittle-tattle and went off to find out more about life in Kinkers. I was looking for Westerton, a farm to the west of the village.

Fraser said that Westerton was an example of the decay of our upland villages in Aberdeenshire. He added that there were plenty more. A woman who was still living there in June 1920 said she had seen 'sixteen reekin' lums in Westerton. Fraser said that there were 'remains of dwellings all about and the shoemaker's and tailor's shops are well within memory'. Most of the houses mentioned by Fraser, or their ruins, had vanished. It was hard to believe that it was once described as 'a considerable hamlet'.

There was another local hamlet that found a place in the history books – Cochran's Croft. It happened when James V – 'the poor man's king' – came to Deeside. Disguised and calling himself the 'gudeman of Ballengeich' he travelled about the country finding out how the people of his realm lived. When his party was approaching Kincardine O'Neil the king wanted to avoid attention, so they stopped at a small roadside croft east of the village. The crofter, Cochran, gave him a warm welcome and the king was so pleased that he granted him the croftland. For many years the name Cochran's Croft appeared on the door of the house, even after it had become became part of the village. Sadly, the name eventually disappeared.

The folk of Kinkers take a delight in odd names. Not far from Cochran's is a hill called Ord Fundlie, which seems to have baffled even the experts. One thought it should be Ord Finlay and another that it meant 'a round hammer-shaped knoll'. But one of my favourite stories is about a man called John Grant, who bought the estate of Kincardine O'Neil in 1780 and erected a mansion house that he called Kincardine Lodge. The house stands on the slope of a ridge on an elevated position about half a mile east of the village. It is an impressive name, Kincardine Lodge, but local folk remembered that the new owner had been a tailor and gave it another name, 'Needle Ha'. He wasn't the first Deeside laird whose property gained an odd name. When George Coates of the Paisley sewing-cotton firm acquired Glentanar House it became known as 'Pirn Ha'. ('Pirn' means a spool of sewing thread, and 'ha' means a hall.)

My wanderings took me to the old ford road that ran down the west side of the church to the river. The ferry crossed farther upstream. The ford was called Cochran's Ford after Cochran's Croft. The boathouse and 'Ferry Cottage' were on the south side of the river. A local man once told me that he could remember when you whistled across the water for the ferryman.

Drovers coming down from the north by Alford and Lumphanan rested their herds at Bartle or Barthol Muir, about a quarter of a mile north of the village. In the 1790s thousands of cattle were sold at the Barthol Fair each year. It must have been some spectacle. They came from far and wide for the fair, crowding the main street of the village and spilling on to the kirkyard. They carried creels and baggage, tethered their horses to the side of the church or let them loose among the graves. They erected tents and booths and, it was recorded, 'exposed their wares upon the graves of the dead'. It was said that 'greater indecencies followed at night'.

So that was Kinkers two centuries ago. Today, there are no cattle bellowing through the village, no armies stripping the village of its food, no cock-stools or ducking-pools keeping scolds and limmers in order – well, not that I saw.

18

BARON OF GARTLY

The village of Clatt hides away at the foot of the Coreen Hills, two miles east of Rhynie. It is aptly named, for the Gaelic word for it is *cleithe*, which means 'concealed'. It may be a tiny, out-of-the-way place, but it has an interesting history. In 1501 it was made into a free burgh of barony by James IV. It had a market cross and it had its own provost and bailies. But some say Clatt was put on the map for another reason – it was the birthplace of the Bard of Corgarff. That may not have made little Clatt famous overnight, but it eventually did wonders for the Allargue Arms, the local hostelry at Corgarff. Here, tourists sipped their drams and goggled at the bard, a local farmer called Wullie Gray, who scribbled dialect poetry on old envelopes and recited it to them. He would tell them he was 'taking the literature to the literati'. His most popular poem, 'The Motor Bike', was about what happened when he took a girl for a spin on a motorbike. They say it matched any of Burns' bawdy poems and Wullie claimed it gave him an international reputation. Visitors from abroad took it down on their cassette recorders and carried it off for the edification of the folks at home.

There was a lad ca'd Willie Gray
He took aff on his motor bike one day
He met a lass and said to her
'Come on doon the road for jist a birr.'
She said to Wull, 'It would be a treat

To hurl on your pillion seat.'
So on she sat as bold as brass
She was a real good-looking lass
Wull thocht that he was gie smart
To hurl aboot wi' this young tart.

They said to her, 'Tuck in yer sark
This bike canna get aff its mark.'
Syne off it took at sic a rate
She slipped on to the number plate
On this sharp point she then did sit –
It ripped her drawers fae head to fit.

There was another man in Clatt who tried to take the literature to the literati, but failed miserably. His lack of success was recorded on his epitaph:

Beneath this stane upon this knowe
Lies single-handed Sandy Low,
He wrote a book nae man could read,
Noo book and author baith are deid.

I used to wonder if there was a real-life Sandy Low, but I never found out.

I thought that our two worthies made up the sum total of Clatt's literary talent, that there were no more poets lurking about in the byres and bothies. But I was wrong. I discovered another Clatt poet who made his mark long before Sandy or Wullie were touched by the Muse. He was the dominie of Clatt School and his name was William Robertson.

I doubt if he would have approved of Wullie Gray's raw verse, for he was a minister of the Kirk. He graduated at King's College in 1804, studied theology in Edinburgh, became dominie at Clatt, and in 1816 went to Angus as minister of the kirk at Carmylie. It was said about his time in Clatt that he did useful service in 'teaching the young idea how to shoot'.

William Robertson was born at Gartly, some four miles north of Clatt, in 1785. There was a railway station there in the days of the Great North of Scotland Railway, but no trains whistle through it now. The village lies north of the well-known Tap o' Noth. There are Noths all over the area, scattered about like blown seed: the Glen of Noth, Old Noth, New Noth, Bogs of Noth, Milton of Noth, and the Hill o' Noth. There is also the Raws of Noth, an extinct hamlet.

Tap o' Noth

The official grid reference of the Raws is 51763105 and there are still some foundations. It is shown on an Ordnance Survey map of 1867 as being around nine rectangular buildings. A map of twenty-one years later shows one of the buildings demolished. It appears to be rough grazing ground now. The word 'raws' simply means rows. Not so long ago the old folk in Huntly spoke of the Raws as houses in the town's Old Road, halfway between the Water of Bogie and the Square.

The word Noth, however, is different; for nobody is quite sure what *it* means. It is said that at one time it meant all the sloping land, several miles in length, along the west side of the Bogie below Rhynie. But the last word lay with William Alexander in his *Place-Names of Aberdeenshire*. He said that 'attempts made to explain it, from the Gael *nochd*, naked, exposed, and the like, are mere ingenuity'. Wullie Gray would have written a pungent verse or two about a naked Gartly exposing itself. Here, in this corner of Strathbogie, the place-names taunt and torment you. The Bogie itself isn't what it seems. The old name of the stream was Bolgyn, whose root was *bolg*, 'a sack or bag,' generally a leather bag. So Bolgyn or Strathbolgyn was 'the stream of the little sacks or bags'. But what did *that* mean? 'The wildest guessing,' wrote James Macdonald, 'will never help us to discover how such names have originated.'

Gartly, like Clatt, is an Aberdeenshire barony. About the middle of the twelfth century it belonged to the Barclays, who were descended from John de Berkeley of Berkeley Castle, in the time of William the Conquerer. They came to Scotland and settled in Gartly about the same time as the Gordons and Leslies. They were a powerful family, powerful enough to have the barony taken away from Aberdeenshire and incorporated in Banffshire. The *New Statistical Account* in 1836 gave the background to this move: 'This anomaly is said to have arisen from the circumstance that the proprietor of the barony, Baron Barclay, one of the feudal barons of the ancient Earls of Huntly, being Sheriff of the County of Banff, used means to get his domains within his own jurisdiction.' The re-alignment of boundaries in May 1891 put an end to this and the barony was back in Aberdeenshire. The barony was where the Barclays of Gartly ruled the roost from the twelfth to the sixteenth centuries. Gartly, or Grantully (there has been a variety of names), was the 'town of the knoll'. In the *Retours of Services* in 1638 there is a reference to the 'lands and barony of Gartullie, comprehending Mains of Gartullie, commonly called Hiltoune'. The Mains was always known as the hill toun, the farm on the hill, on the east side of the Bogie on the edge of the great sprawl of Clashindarroch Forest.

There are some intriguing place names in the barony, among them the Buried Men's Leys. Who the buried men were I never found out, but near this gloomy spot is the site of the Piper's Cairn, where a piper returning from Harlaw fell and was buried. There was another piper I was interested in – a shepherd playing his 'rustic pipe' in Gartly Castle. I read about him in a song that began:

Frae Gartly Castle's auld grey wa',
Where lords hae dwelt an' lairds an' a',
A shepherd by that haunted ha',
Wi' your guid pleasure,
Wad mint his rustic pipe to blaw
In doric measure.

The man who wrote that song was the dominie-cleric from Clatt, William Robertson, who acquired a love for vernacular poetry when wandering about the brooding hills of Strathbogie. Reared in a district that was rich in legendary and ballad lore, he had little difficulty in finding subjects for his pen. The Barons of Gartly had long since slipped into the shadows, but they were never forgotten, and Robertson had this in mind when he returned to the 'haunted ha'' on the banks of the Bogie.

Many of his songs and ballads were written between 1804 and 1835. In 1835 a poem called 'Sang o' the Starvin' Poet' appeared anonymously in *Chambers Journal* and in 1884 it appeared again under the title of 'The Waeful Want o' Siller' in the *Free Press*. Some thought it was the work of Burns. It is the story of what happens to a hard-up poet when his 'siller' runs out:

> There's unco few will look yer way
> Gin that the siller be na kythin'. [is not appearing]
> Fat is't, think ye, locks hands an' hearts?
> It's neither beauty, wit, nor carriage,
> But frae the cottage tae the ha'
> It's siller aye that mak's the marriage.
> I've been in love out o-er the lugs,
> As lovin' hearts o' nature's lythin [soothing]
> Haill beuks I've writ, baith verse and prose,
> An' mony a roozin' dedication;
> Yet nae ane owned the poor bauch chiel, tired-out [tired-out fellow]
> An' noo there's naught but grim starvation.

Whether or not Robertson's 'Sang o' the Starvin' Poet' was based on his own experience as a young poet is anybody's guess, yet it is interesting that up to 1835 he wrote more than twenty pieces – songs, epistles and ballads – but, like the 'poor bauch chiel' in his poem, he never received the recognition due to him. His poems, it was said, 'passed from mouth to mouth and soon became undistinguishable from the older anonymous productions which everybody could sing, but of which few knew the origin'.

In 1823, Alex Laing, a well-known chapman, better known as 'Stachie' Laing, or sometimes as Gley'd Sandy because of his squint, published *Thistle of Scotland,* a collection of ancient ballads. Among them was a ballad called 'The Baron of Gartly'. Laing had no idea who wrote it. He had probably taken it down from the singing or recitation of someone in Aberdeenshire, and he came to the conclusion that it dated from the sixteenth century. Laing, unaware that the author was still alive, and still producing poems, praised the ballad. He thought it was 'very good for the age it has been wrote in, free from the turgid stiffness accompanying a

great many of the ancient songs. It bears every mark of being the work of
the sixteenth century, owing to the reigning chimeras of spectres and
wizards.' Robertson was brought up on stories of witches and bogles and
the antics of Auld Nick. In one of his early poems, 'Nannie', he said what
he would do if 'onie cunnin' worthless chiel contrive my Nannie's charms
to steal'. He would put the 'muckle horn'd diel' on to him so that he would
'rive the filthy tyke in twa'. But Gartly's 'bauld and burly Baronne' was the
Clatt dominie's fearful masterpiece. I'll end this chapter with the opening
stanzas of the ballad, in which he is introduced:

Twas at midnight's darkest hour.
Nae moon nor stars gave light,
When Gartley's bauld and burly Baronne
Rode homeward through the night.

Sturdy was that Baronne's spear –
Deadly his battle brand;
Could nae man bide aneath the stroke
O' his uplifted hand.

Frae his war cap three feathers black
Nod o'er his dark brent brow; [smooth]
Durst nae man speir where he them gat,
Or he had cause to rue.

His mail o' steel frae neck to heel,
Wi' witchin' spell was bound;
Twas clasped sae fast, war's deadliest blast
Could ne'er that Baronne wound.

19

BEND-UP-HIGH

Alexander Robb, respected Aberdeen merchant, tailor, wit, poet, politician and deacon of the Tailors' Incorporation, struggled up over the last few rocky yards of his ascent of Bennachie and emerged triumphant on the summit of the Mither Tap. He had come up out of the rich gold of the Garioch, leaving behind the castles and woods, and now, looking down the 'glorious girnal of the North' he wondered why other poets had never sung the praises of the 'mighty mountain' of Bennachie. It might have been different if Walter Scott or Robert Burns had stood there. If that had happened the whole world would have heard or read about it. Later, he wrote the lines:

Shall Deeside hills be fam'd afar
In history's pages, and tuneful lays –
Shall thy dark mountain, Lochnagar,
Excite the Lordl'y Poet's praise?
And shall thy mountains, lovely Don
Entice no Bard to sing of thee?
'Mong Scotia's Minstrels is there none
To sing of lofty Bennachie?

There were, in fact, poets who had sung of Bennachie long before Deacon Robb appeared on the scene. Not least among them was Arthur Johnston, from Caskieben, the seventeenth-century Latinist and poet who became rector of King's College, Old Aberdeen. Johnston found time to write, in Latin, a poem in honour of his birthplace, and in it he saw the Garioch in much the same terms as the deacon: waving fields of yellow corn, proud castles, herds grazing in wanton meadows, ruddy apples on bending boughs, and, above all else:

> Here, towering high, Bennachie spreads
> Around in all his evening shades,
> When twilight gray comes on;
> With sparkling gems the river glows,
> As in the east are known.

More than three and a half centuries later they are still writing about Bennachie. Deacon Robb's fears have been allayed in a way he could never have foreseen, for in the years since he first scrambled ecstatically up the Mither Tap it has been drowned in a deluge of words. Whatever Byron did for Lochnagar, a thousand lesser-known writers have done in far greater measure for this noted peak on the northern rim of the Grampians. It is without doubt the hill of the poets. It evokes and provokes emotions that strangers must often find hard to understand. No one, for instance, can readily explain the impulse that once made over a hundred people tramp

Bennachie – The Mither Tap in the background

up the hill to spout Doric as if they were chanting some weird Druid litany. Perhaps it was a hark back to those far-off days. It was once said that Bennachie derived its name from Beinn-a-Che, meaning the mountain of Che, a pagan deity, and the Pictish chronicles told of Cruithe, King of the Picts, dividing among his seven sons the country north of the Forth and Clyde. One of them was Che, who ruled Mar and Buchan.

Most people, however, think that the name means 'hill of the paps', although this was dismissed by James Macdonald, author of *Place-Names of West Aberdeenshire* (1899), as 'totally inadmissible'. He may have been influenced by his Victorian sense of propriety, unlike Dr Maitland Mackie, who once admitted feeling deliciously naughty reciting Charles Murray's lines about the Paps of Bennachie. Macdonald put his money on a derivation from *ceathach*, 'mist'. Beinn a Cheathaich, 'hill of the mist', or Beinn a Chiithe, 'hill of the rain'. Those who know the Mither Tap and its moods are not likely to argue with this: 'When Bennachie pits on its tap/ The Garioch lads will get a drap.'

The last word on the subject should probably be left to P Finlayson, one of those travellers who wandered about the country in the eighteenth and nineteenth centuries putting down their thoughts on the heathen Scot. Finlayson, who was known as 'the observing farmer', published his *Travels Through Scotland* in 1834. His explanation of the name Bennachie may not have a Johnsonian profundity but, surrounded by Pagan deities, ceathachs and ciths, it is difficult to quarrel with someone whose simple logic told him that 'Benahee' should really be 'Ben-up-High'. 'There is a hill in the Garioch called Benahee,' he wrote, 'but the proper name is Ben-up-high. It rises almost perpendicular in the southeast and is very high. There is an excellent quarry on top of it, containing beautiful granite. It is out of that quarry the stone was taken for George the Fourth's monument in Edinburgh.' Finlayson ended up misspelling the 'proper name' and printed it as Bend-up-high: 'Many of the Bend-up-high stones are sent to London.'

In 1654, Robert Gordon of Straloch described Bennachie as precipitous, rocky, rising with seven tops, and acting as a 'sea mark'. It is also, as a familiar couplet tells us, very much a landmark. Travelling about the North-east, you see its distinctive outline at almost every turn, sharp and clear against the summer sky and, as Johnny Gibb of Gushetneuk put it, 'as fite's a washen fleece' when there are 'oorlich (cold) shoo'ers o' drift an' hail scoorin' across the kwintra'.

W Douglas Simpson's description of Bennachie as the sphinx of the

Garioch suggests an incomparable timelessness. It is a staggering thought that the granite forming the Bennachie ridge is something like 400 million years old, but even that extraordinary fact will not persuade people away from the view expressed by the poet Flora Garry in one of her poems, 'Foo aul's Bennachie'.

> 'Foo aul's Bennachie? As aul's a man?'
> Loon-like I wid speir, an leave my bools [marbles]
> A boorach in the kypie at my feet [heap, hole]
> An stan' an stare oot ower the darknin' lan'
> Ower parks and ferms, as far's my een could see
> To the muckle hill aneth the settin sun.
> 'Aul'er, laddie, aye, gin Man himsel'
> Naebody kens the age o' Bennachie'.

It is a hill that inspires a fierce possessiveness. In an introduction to *The Book of Bennachie*, the late Lord Aberdeen declared, 'The hell with your Alps, Rockies and Himalay. Bennachie is the hill for me.' Charles Murray's comparisons were with less awe-inspiring peaks, but his sentiments were the same:

> There's Tap o' Noth, the Buck, Ben Newe,
> Lonach, Benrinnes, Lochnagar,
> Mount Keen, an' mony a Cairn I trow
> That's smored in mist ayont Braemar.
> Bauld Ben Muich Dhui towers, until
> Ben Nevis looms the laird o' a';
> But Bennachie! Faith, yon's the hill
> Rugs at the hairt when ye're awa'!

The exile clings tenaciously to his memories of the Mither Tap, unwilling to cut the umbilical cord. Lord Aberdeen thought of Bennachie when frozen on the plains of northern France and frizzled in the sands of Egypt. The sound of a piper playing 'The Back o' Bennachie', he said, 'induced the most appalling nostalgia'. Charles Murray, sitting at starlit banquets thousands of miles from home, could think only of wading through the bracken on Bennachie.

Wherever the exiles were, there was always the hope that one day they would be 'rivin' on up Bennachie again. Some never returned. One of

Hamewith's most moving poems was 'In Lythe Strathdon':

> Seldom a simmer passed but him an' me
> Amang the hills had some fine cheery days,
> Up Nochtyside or throu' the Cabrach braes,
> Doon the Lord's Throat, an' ootower Bennachie;
> There wasna mony bare hill-heads onkent to him an' me.

> Never nae mair. I wander noo my leen,
> An' he's been beddit lang in far Peronne;
> Here, whaur his forbears lie in lythe Strathdon,
> I lay the stag-moss that I pu'ed yestreen –
> Laurels fae Lonach, where I range oor auld hill tracks my leen.

If a lad went off to what Flora Garry called 'the onchancy wardle furth o' Bennachie' it wasn't necessary to travel to distant, alien lands to feel the homeward pull of Bennachie. There was no place more alien than the frenetic, traffic-ridden streets of Glasgow, where they had mountains of stone climbing up to the heavens. J Pittendreigh McGillivray, King's Limner for Scotland and a Port Elphinstone man, was one of those poets who itched to flee from the 'hell o' shops an' motor cars in Glasgow' and back to the Mither Tap. His poem 'In Exile' carried these lines:

> Up at the back o' Bennachie
> Faur Gaudie rins sae sweet,
> Gin I were there I'd be at hame
> An off the hard steen street.

A number of songs have been written about the streams that run through Bennachie's land, but the Gadie is the best known, although it is not a stream from which dreams are made. Writer Alex Inkson McConnochie in his book *Bennachie* said it was 'not such a beautiful stream as might fairly be expected from its almost world-wide reputation'. More bluntly, the poet William Thom described it as 'a desperately crabbed-looking rivulet, raging and rumbling from Bennachie'. Be that as it may, it put Bennachie on the map.

John Imlah, one of the eighteenth-century 'Bards of Bon-Accord', made the Gadie song his own with the words he put to the exquisite melody. The lines generally attributed to him are these:

The Gadie Burn

O gin I were where Gadie rins,
Where Gadie rins, where Gadie rins,
 O gin I were where Gadie rins,
At the back o' Bennachie.

I've roamed by Tweed, I've roamed by Tay,
By Border Nith and Highland Spey,
But dearer far to me than they
The braes o' Bennachie.

John Imlah was the son of Peter Imlah, an innkeeper from Cuminestone in
Buchan. A century and a half after the poet's death a group was set up in
the Garioch called the Bailies of Bennachie, whose self-imposed task was

to act as custodians of the hill which inspired the Gadie ballad. There are still bailies there today, keeping watch on the hill and the hundreds of people who tramp over it.

Of all the characters who swagger across the pages of Bennachie's colourful story, none can match the mighty Jock o' Bennachie. He was a giant among giants and the only man who could look him in the eye was Jock o' Noth, who was of similar build. When they came together they were 'twa grisly sights to see':

There were three feet between their brows,
And shoulders were yards three.

Even giants like Jock o' Bennachie have their ups and downs. Life became 'unco dreich and dreary' for Jock until he met a 'lady fair' on Bennachie and was so captivated by her wistful look that he raised her up and kissed her. There was 'a maist unearthly licht' and Jock and his lady sank down through the hill, out of sight.

Keep your eyes open the next time you are up by the Mither Tap. Who knows, you might see them walking hand-in-hand on the Bend-up-high.

In 1872, Queen Victoria, going north from Aberdeen, recorded in her diary that the royal train went 'past Inverurie, close past the hill of Bennachie'. She may well have peeped up at the Mither Tap and wondered what it was like to stand on top of it. The Queen Mother certainly did. During a visit to Aberdeen in 1940, when she was queen consort, the lord provost, Sir Thomas Mitchell, showed her Bennachie. 'I wish we had been going up there!' she said.

20

THE OLD BROWN HILLS

It's a warm wind, the west wind, full of birds' cries
I never hear the west wind but tears are in my eyes.
For it comes from the west lands, the old brown hills,
And April's in the west wind, and daffodils.

from 'The West Wind', John Masefield

When John Hardyng, the English chronicler and mapmaker, visited
Scotland in 1418 he saw the 'goodly cytee' of Aberdeen – and passed
through 'all the mountaynes wher the wild Scottes do dwel'. Those early
discoverers, men like John Taylor, the Water Poet; Thomas Pennant, the
traveller and naturalist; Edward Burt, chief surveyor to General Wade; and
that incomparable duo Johnson and Boswell, were intrigued by the people,
amused by their customs and fascinated by the countryside, but most of
all they were awed and elated by the great mountain ranges, the old brown
hills, spreading their ridges and furrows across the face of Scotland.

Not all were complimentary. The mountains, wrote Edward Burt in
1725, had 'the disagreeable appearance of a scabbed head,' and the
acerbic Dr Johnson, while impressed with the wild scenery on his tour of
Scotland in 1773, refused to be swept off his feet. When Boswell described
one mountain as immense, Johnson tartly corrected him. 'No!' he said, 'It
is no more than a considerable protuberance.' But that was high praise
from a man who had an ill-concealed prejudice against Scotland, and for
the most part the early travellers were enchanted. In 1618, John Taylor, a
guest of 'my good Lord of Marr' burst into verse about 'skie-kissing
mountains, craggy cliffs and thunder-battered hills,' and in 1769 Thomas
Pennant waxed eloquent about 'sublime mountainous scenery' and the
'majestic grandeur of summits'.

Ninety years later, Queen Victoria, who became more Scottish than the Scots, put her seal of approval on it when she climbed Deeside's Morven on her pony and wrote in her diary, 'Such seas of mountains . . . so wonderfully beautiful.' That did it. If, as Dr Johnson had said, the noblest prospect a Scot ever saw was the high road leading to England, today he would face an inordinate amount of traffic going in the opposite direction.

Meanwhile the wild Scots followed their usual habit of seeing all and saying little. If they had any thoughts about their native hills they had some difficulty in expressing them, at least at their own firesides. W Douglas Simpson, in *The Highlands of Scotland*, said that when a man left his native glen or mountainside he retained, wherever he might settle or however long his exile, a haunting, affectionate memory of the scenes of his childhood. At home he might even seem indifferent to the beauty or grandeur of his surroundings; elsewhere his nostalgia often displayed itself in a vigorous championship of his own district or shire as the most beautiful in all the Highlands.

Scots writers have rarely indulged in the panegyric prose with which the English described the hills. One reason for this was suggested as far back as 1824. In a preface to *The Aberdeenshire Lintie*, the compiler wrote 'Heath-clad mountains and murmuring streams are all very fine in their way for those who have time and opportunity to climb the heathery steps of the one, or repose under the fragrant boughs of another, and while they may, in a great measure, tend to nurture the "divine germ", yet there is much silly, sickly affectation whispered about regarding them. Nine-tenths of those who had produced anything deserving of the name of poetry had little opportunities of studying the beauties of nature.'

This was not the case at the turn of the twentieth century, when North-east poets like Charles Murray began to emerge from their creative chrysalis. If, as Byron once said, high mountains are a feeling, Murray had a complete understanding of what that meant. Moreover, he was able to express it in the language of the North-east and relate it to ordinary folk. Today, the ghost of *Hamewith* must smile down on the Mither Tap when it sees the unending stream of people puffing uphill from the heart of 'Garioch'.

'What a roll-call he gives of our Northern hills,' wrote Nan Shepherd, but she herself was to produce a work of great sensitivity about the Cairngorms, a richly evocative piece of writing that lay in a drawer for thirty years until she was persuaded to publish it in 1977. Still, as Miss Shepherd said in a foreword to *The Living Mountain*, 'thirty years in the life of a mountain is nothing – the flicker of an eyelid'.

She wrote, too, in the Doric about the harsh and desolate high lands, about dark Loch Avon and the caul', caul' waters running under the snow on Ben a' Bhuird. With such writers our northern hills were in good hands, and there was little fear of slipping back into a 'hill and dale' culture when a poet like John C Milne could gaze on the awful immensity of the Cairngorms and sum it up in two words: 'Gey hulls.'

Gey hills they are, but the little hills also have their place. It may be that they touch slumbering chords of nostalgia more easily than the great peaks. They shrink distance, stirring memory's images for the exile wearying for home at the other side of the world. Charles Murray described how, by night and day, his dream was the same, of a world at peace in which he would be back where a burn sunk 'saft-oxtered' into the Don, away from danger, din and stir, 'back to the quiet hills'.

The hills, too, are a bridge between childhood and old age. George MacDonald, the Huntly poet and novelist, who died at the beginning of last century, wrote a great deal for children, and one of his poems, 'The Hills', looked back to the days when his 'childhood's busy feet' ran up the little grassy brae behind his house, where he could look down in wonder on the chimneys of the town.

> Around the house, where'er I turned,
> Great hills closed up the view;
> The town midst their converging arms
> Was clasped by rivers two;
> From one hill to another sprang
> The sky's great arch of blue.

Huntly was identified in MacDonald's mind by its hills, and this is true of many places in the North-east. Buchan is Mormond, the Garioch is the Mither Tap, and the bleak lands of the Cabrach would be no different from any other moory wilderness if someone was able to flatten the noble Buck.

Most people admire the hills from ground level, but more and more are being tempted upwards, which gives rise to ominous mutterings about danger, which of course there is, and about heavy-booted feet creating erosion, which must be a tiny thing compared with the unthinking mauling of the hills by the bulldozers of gun-shooting lairds.

Nan Shepherd said of the climber 'Aye the warld cries oot on him for fey [fate].' John M. Caie confessed in *The Hill Climber* that there were times when he thought he was 'daft tae dee't'. But Caie, sweating and peching, his feet on fire, knew there was reward at the end:

> Though winds may roar an' rain may drive,
> Wi' squelchin' sheen an' scratit knees
> Ye haud on, kennin' that belyve, [soon]
> Ye'll hairst a gran', a noble crap, [harvest] [groan] [crop]
> For, oh, the glory at the tap!
> But perhaps we are bewitched.

JC Milne, who took second place to none in his affection for the hills, nevertheless had moments when he thought of the broad, flat lands of his native Buchan and wondered if by leaving them he had also taken leave of his senses. He went up Lochnagar and declared:

> God bless Buchan, braid and gweed!
> And God bless me, I've muckle need!
> For, man, I've connached a' my queet [spoiled] [ankle]
> And blistered baith my fairmin feet!

Walk the hills and you will often come upon cairns in memory of people who loved them, or lost their lives in them, or wanted their ashes scattered amongst them. On a stretch of Rothiemurchus moor, against the backcloth of the Cairngorms, there is a cairn to Hugh Alexander Barrie, who, with a friend, Thomas Baird, lost his life in a Cairngorm blizzard in 1928. The previous year Barrie had written a poem which prophetically expressed the wish that when he was dead he would be given 'a windswept boulder for a bier', so that he would still know the lash of rain, the savage bellowing of stags, and the embrace of the rushing wind.

JC Milne touched on this subject in two of his poems, 'Faur wid I Dee' and 'Coire an Dubh Lochan'. In the first he looked askance at the idea of dying in the heart of a town 'streekit oot straucht in a dark kist'. He wanted to be buried in Beinn a Bhuird or Ben A'an, 'faur there's a scowth [scope] for the Lord to tak' yer spirit in han''. In the second he asked:

> Hap me up weel,
> But nae owre weel for ilka noo 'n 'an
> I wid like to be wi' the ongauns and the steer, [goings on] [bustle]
> Wind on Dubh Lochan, thunder owre Ben A'an,
> And the reid hull deer.

Sadly, he was buried in an Aberdeen cemetery.

JM Caie's native caution about such ongoings asserted itself. 'Bury me here, bury me there,' he said, 'sic daft-like notions fowk gets i' their heid o faur they'd be pitten efter they're deid.' It didn't make any difference to him what happened to his body when he was dead. Still, when he thought of the millions and millions of people from all the ages who had gone through the gates of Heaven, a quiet neuk might be hard to find in Paradise. Perhaps, after all, a lone hilltop would suit him:

Beery me, then, fin comes the time,
Hine an' heich in a rocky grave, [far away and high]
Far the win's gyang soochin' or roarin' by
An' the wild birds wheel 'neth the open sky.
An' noo, gin ye say't, I canna deny
That I'm jist as daft as the lave. [the rest]

21

TREE OF GOLD

The road that runs through Glen Luibeg from Derry Lodge in the Cairngorms skirts a hill called Carn Crom. The name means 'a bent or crooked hill,' which is not a bad description of it, but above it is a ridge of rocks known as Coire na Saobhaidhe, the corrie of the fox's den. The place-name expert William Alexander gave it a translation that was even scarier, 'the corrie of the wild beast's den'.

Whether or not these names have ever made climbers think twice about going up Carn Crom I have no idea, but this bent and crooked hill stands sentinel over Craobh an Oir – the Tree of Gold. For centuries, people have believed there is – or was – a treasure buried on the hill. They still come looking for it.

There have been many curious tales told about the Tree of Gold, but the most reliable came from that doyen of the hills, Seton Gordon, in his book *The Cairngorm Hills of Scotland,* published in 1925. Gordon heard the story of the Tree of Gold from John Macintosh, a piper, who came from Inverey. Macintosh was one of a coterie of estate workers who knew him, among them Donald Fraser, who played golf with him in a clearing at Derry Lodge, and Charles Robertson, who tamed mice in the Corrour bothy.

Gordon told how the laird of Dalmore (now Mar Lodge) had been raiding in Lochaber and had brought back a considerable amount of treasure. He decided to bury it in Garbh Choire Dhe, a deep corrie lying in the great gulf separating Braeriach from Cairn Toul. In the short December days it was 'often a place of whirling snows, of drift so dense that it is impossible even to see against it, and almost impossible to draw breath in the face of the storm,' so the laird changed his mind. He moved it to Glen Lui Beg.

One of the oldest trees in the forest stood far up the hillside of Carn Crom and it was there that the laird's gold was buried – at Craobh an Oir, the Tree of Gold. Some years later the laird decided to move the treasure again. He had heard that land in Cromar was for sale and he made up his mind to buy some of it with his treasure. Cromar was not the lovely haugh it is now – I had a caravan there for many years – and when the laird got to the top of Culblean and looked down on it he saw an expanse of bog and loch. '*No leigeadh Dia gun cuireadh mise mor san*', 'May God forbid that I should throw my gold into the water,' he said.

'He turned homeward with his treasure,' wrote Gordon, 'and hid it this time near the top of Cairn Geldie. He placed over the "pan" containing it a huge stone whereon was carved the figure of a horse's shoe. And there, according to tradition, it remains to this day.'

Nobody, as far as I know, goes searching the Geldie moors for a stone with a carved horseshoe on top of it, but the possibility of finding hidden treasure still draws the people to Luibeg. Not long ago I saw an online report by a party from the University of Northumbria Mountaineering Club on a visit to what they called the Dalmore Gold. Another report came from two families who camped at a burn opposite Coire Craobh an Oir. In the evening they wandered up to the Craobh. There were no wild beasts there, but they were attacked by an army of midges. Two other gold hunters said they would be back with spades.

The Cairngorms are a vast, open book. The old tales are everywhere, magnified by the names seen on maps, or heard in bothy talk, tongue-twisting names, often unfathomable, sometimes frightening, frequently unreadable, occasionally romantic. Seton Gordon pondered on such names when he stood at the summit of Cairn of Braeriach and saw 'the most wild and *romantic* spot' of all the Cairngorm hills. A few feet from the cairn the ground fell away. There was a drop of almost 1,500 feet and 'this great and wonderful precipice' was Coire Brochain, also known as the Corrie of the Porridge.

'How curious a name to give the corrie – Coire Bhrochain – the Corrie of the Porridge!' said Seton Gordon. 'What, one wonders, is its history? There is a tradition amongst some of the older stalkers of the Forest of Mar that once, long ago, a herd of cattle crossing the Lairig Ghru – that ancient track between Dee and Spey – eluded the drovers and in some way scaled the heights of Brae Riach. In the thick mist they lost their heads, and fell from the hill-top over that dizzy height, so that when found they were crushed to a pulp of the consistency of *brochan* or porridge.'

Gordon said he had written too much about the Corries of Braeriach – he gave over a whole chapter to them – and felt he had little space to describe the beauties of other corries. He was something of a place-name buff, digging out curious names like Coire Both-cloiche, the 'Corrie of the Stone Bothy' – there is an old stone ruin below it – the Horseman's Corrie, from a Mr Horseman who often stalked stags there, and the mysterious Coire Dhondail. Gordon was told it was a corruption of Gamhandail, the Corrie of the Dale of the Stirks. In the days of the summer shielings young cattle pastured on its sweet grass.

A flat-topped boulder called Clachan Nan Taillear stands beside the Lairig Ghru at the base of Carn a Mhaim. This is the Tailors' Stone, where three tailors perished one winter long ago. When they set off they said they would dance at the 'three dells'. They danced at two of them, the Dell of Abernethy and the Dell of Rothiemurchus, but a blizzard of snow overtook them and they died in the shelter of the stone that carries their names.

The third dell was Dalmore, home of the laird with the hidden gold. Dalmore – Dail Mhor, the big haugh – is now Mar Lodge. The man with the Tree of Gold was a Fraser, but there is nothing to show which one. The Dail Mhor was first mentioned in the fifteenth century when it was granted to Kenneth Mackenzie, son of Kenneth Mackenzie of Kintail in Wester Ross, by King James IV. He was the first to build a 'lodge' there. Dalmore was in the heart of the Forest of Mar and the Mackenzies were foresters to the earls of Mar. After the 1715 Jacobite Rising the Mackenzies ran into financial difficulties and sold Dalmore to Lords Dun and Grange, but in the 1730s the property was acquired by the Duffs.

There have been three Mar Lodges. The first was a plain structure behind the present building, followed in the middle of the nineteenth century by a new mansion at Corriemulzie across the River Dee. They called it New Mar Lodge, but it was described as a 'shapeless old hunting lodge with verandas supported by rustic tree trunks'. I carried a picture of it in *A Queen's Country* and it seemed to be full of old-world charm. At any rate, it had a special appeal: a remarkable collection of stags' heads, some perched on the roof of the building.

New Mar Lodge was destroyed by fire in 1895. Many of the stags' heads were saved and now decorate the present Mar Lodge, which was

Bynack

completed in 1898. I saw them six years ago when I was shown around the lodge by Mrs Sandra Dempster, the housekeeper. I remember walking through the stately corridors of the lodge feeling as if I was being watched by dozens of eyes. They were stags' eyes, blinking at me from 'stuffed' deer heads that hung from almost every wall in the lodge.

Some of the heads had tags on them. The name of John Paunchaud was on one of the tags. He and his brother Gerald were Swiss. They bought the estate in 1961 and sold it later to an American billionaire, John Kluge, who eventually sold it to the National Trust. The tag on John Paunchaud's trophy indicated that he had made his 'kill' on Beinn Bhrochain – the Corrie of the Porridge!

There were five luxurious apartments in Mar Lodge – Derry, Macdui, Dalvorar, Braeriach, and Bynack. All these names I knew, but the name Bynack struck special chords for me. Now a ruin, it was a well-known lodge just south of the Geldie, where Queen Victoria took her leave of the Duke of Atholl when returning from Blair Castle. The name, however, meant more to me than an old shiel – it brought to mind the legendary Nell Bynack. Her real name was Helen Macdonald, but nobody ever called her that; she got her by-name, like the rest of her family, because she spent her childhood at Bynack.

Mar lodge today

Her father, Sandy Macdonald, was gamekeeper there and she knew the hills like the back of her hand. She once told me with a laugh, 'I'm hill run'. That other legendary lady of the hills, Maggie Gruer, fed and bedded Cairngorm walkers, but Nell had higher aims – she was an unofficial guide to hotel guests and climbed to the top of Ben Macdhui twenty-two times. She eventually moved to Luibeg, and Seton Gordon often stayed with her there.

Mar Lodge is a magnificent salute to the past, but all around it are reminders of a way of life that has long-since disappeared. The ballroom is a grotesque leftover from the old days. It has been dismissed as an 'overgrown chalet' and its style brushed aside as 'suburban Tudor'. It was originally built at Corriemulzie in 1883, but when the present Mar Lodge was built the ballroom was dismantled and moved to its present site in 1898.

There were more stags' eyes winking at me when I went into the ballroom. They didn't seem quite as welcoming as those in the lodge for most of them were skulls, along with some stuffed heads. There were supposed to be 2,500 skulls and stuffed heads on the ceiling, maybe more, for I don't think anyone has climbed up there and counted them. I couldn't help thinking of the laird who, when the lodge was destroyed by fire in 1895, ran about crying, 'Save the stags' heads! Save the stags'

The stag's head ceiling in the ballroom

heads!' Some of those heads were looking pitifully down at me. I thought they were trying to tell me something.

In the late seventeenth century there were a number of townships on the haughs around Mar Lodge, but they were cleared by the Earl of Fife so that he could get a clear view around the lodge. East of Mar Lodge is Allanaquoich, which had five tenants and twelve subtenants in 1696. Farther east, Allanmore has become a 'lost' township. All around the farmhouse are the foundations of earlier buildings.

But it is when you go west, up Glen Lui to Derry Lodge and on again to Luibeg, that the old settlements catch your eye. These are the real 'ghost' towns, these nameless heaps of stones. I once wrote about Glen Lui as a glen of sad memories, its 'lost lands' staked out in rubble heaps along the road to Derry Lodge. Seton Gordon saw the glen as 'almost as deserted as the high Cairngorms'.

22

THE MARATHON WALKER

It was half-past four on a September morning in 1819. William MacGillivray, a 23-year-old student, got out of his bed in Old Aberdeen, breakfasted at five, and set off on a walk. He tramped through the deserted city streets, down King Street to Castle Street and the Shiprow and then out on to the Deeside road. His walk that day ended at Aboyne, thirty miles away. Most people would have regarded it as a gruelling walk, but MacGillivray planned to end it a lot farther on – in London!

In his *Journal* he explained why he had undertaken this marathon hike, a walk of nearly eight hundred miles. 'In London City,' he wrote, 'there is, I am told, a great collection of beasts and fishes and of birds and other flying things, of reptiles and insects – in short, of all the creatures which have been found upon the face of the earth.' He wanted to see them.

Young MacGillivray, who was to become one of the country's leading naturalists, said that his main object in undertaking the journey on foot was to 'extend my knowledge in natural history, which can only be done by travelling'. He had learned that the best way to do that was by shank's mare – his own legs. Born in Old Aberdeen in 1796, he was brought up by relatives in Harris, and at the age of eleven he walked from Harris to Aberdeen to complete his education. Later, his work took him on long tramps into the hills.

The London walk got off to a bad start. He wrote in his *Journal* that when he reached Aboyne he had eaten 'a poor supper and taken a glass of whisky'. He went to bed at eleven and during the night had 'a severe headache and a violent fit of shivering, followed by great heat without sweating'. However, in the morning his headache had gone. After breakfast he went back on the road – he had only 770 miles to go!

He marched on to Braemar and Kingussie, then to Loch Laggan, and on to Fort William, where he stayed for two days. But it was no rest period, for he spent one day climbing Ben Nevis before heading south through Glencoe. He reached Glasgow and marvelled at the steamboats on the Clyde and the streets and houses all lit up by gas. He passed through Paisley and at Ayr shared a bed with some troublesome visitors. 'It had been better for me that I had slept by a hedge,' he wrote, 'for I am almost covered by tumours and vesications produced by the bites of bugs. How gladly I would have exchanged my bed for a couch of grass on the side of Cairngorm.'

He came to Burns country and found the cottage in which Rab was born. It had been turned into a public house. MacGillivray was a Burns fan and, like the Bard, enjoyed a dram; his *Journal* has repeated references to him taking a glass. But in the poet's birthplace he did an extraordinary thing. He drank 'half a mutchkin of the favourite potation of the unfortunate bard' – about half a pint – and then poured the rest on the floor.

'I knelt down upon the floor with my hat off,' he wrote. 'Immortal Burns,' said I aloud, 'here on my knees I do homage to thy genius,' and pouring the liquor upon the floor, added, 'and pour forth this libation to thy memory. Poor fellow! There never was a genius upon earth whose memory is dearer to my heart. Big drops are trickling down my cheeks, I know not why. I cannot scrutinise my feelings. My soul is sad.'

Wiping his tears, he went on his way, through Girvan to Stranraer, Castle Douglas and Dumfries. He spent the night at Dumfries and went in search of Burns' grave. He climbed over a wall of the churchyard and began searching the monuments. He came upon one in the form of a dome, supported by eight Ionic pillars. Through the railings he could see the figure of a man holding a plough in white marble. 'This is it!' he said. He climbed over a stone wall and an iron railing, sat down on the steps, and burst into tears again.

'The only words which broke forth at intervals between my sobs,' he said, 'were "poor unfortunate Burns". I felt that his very memory was dearer to me than any living being of my own sex. I know not what attaches me so closely to this child of nature.' He planned to write his last report while in Scotland in the village of Gretna, but he landed up in a place called Springfield. 'I thought I had come to Gretna,' he wrote, 'and so entered an inn; but on inquiry I found that Gretna is a quarter of a mile off.' 'It is a matter of little consequence,' he said, and consoled himself with a breakfast of twopence-worth of bread – and a gill of whisky!

MacGillivray had £10 in his pocket when he started his walk. He planned to spend half of it on the first half of his journey, the other half on the tramp from the Borders to London, but to achieve that he had to restrict his eating habits. 'I wished to begin a new account on entering England,' he wrote. 'I have now travelled about 500 miles and I have been thirty days on my journey. I have seldom eaten oftener than twice a day, and I have just expended five pounds sterling.'

So over the Border went our marathon walker, sleeping in the loft of a byre one night wet to the knees, putting up the next night in an inn, where he 'deemed it proper and becoming and expedient to recruit my spirits by taking a few drops of the creature. I ordered a gill of rum . . . ' He spent a Sunday at Kendal, where he was shocked 'to see the Sabbath violated by people who profess the Christian religion'. Perhaps it was to soften the shock that he ordered 'a pint of ale and a glass of rum, and a smoke of tobacco'.

There was little doubt that Mr MacGillivray liked his dram. He was also fond of his food, for he decided it was 'needless to torment myself with bad meals'. He said he could bear hunger as well as most people, for he had once travelled 240 miles on 12 shillings. But now there would be no more tuppeny loaves of bread. 'I will indulge my gluttonous appetite,' he declared.

His good spirits began to evaporate when he reached Ashbourne, where he put up at a lodging house for pedlars and Irish vagrants. His fellow lodgers were 'two Irish pedlars, an Italian picture and looking-glass vendor, a Don Quixote shoemaker, a couple of spindle-shanked, lanthorn-jawed creatures, two young girls and a fat bull-dog.' One of his fellow lodgers said he 'would rather encounter Auld Sootie than a parcel of Irish tinkers'. MacGillivray survived the night. He got up before eight, got 'a pennyworth tea and a pennyworth of sugar and twopence worth of bread,' and went on his way.

On Tuesday, 18 October, MacGillivray was sixty miles from London – and his money was down to thirteen pence halfpenny. The road was hard and his shoes and stockings were in tatters. When he was eighteen miles from London he still had threepence ha'penny in his pocket. He got bread and an apple with his 'copper clinkum' [money], and 'crawled along'.

He had to sit down every two or three miles to ease his feet, but he reached Highgate at about twelve o'clock and, soon after, he entered London. There was no triumphant march into the city. The rain poured down in torrents and he was 'wetted to the skin'. He crawled to an address at No. 31 Poultry to pick up a parcel sent from Aberdeen. Then he found lodgings and had 'a glorious snoring bout'. The Great Marathon Walk was over. 'I have now finished my journey,' he wrote in his *Journal,* 'and I am satisfied with my conduct.'

He remained in London for seven days, returning to Aberdeen by steamboat and arriving there on 7 November 1819. He had been away for two months and the distance he had walked was precisely eight hundred and thirty-seven miles.

Two years before his Aberdeen–London jaunt he had whetted his appetite for long-distance walking with a tour through the Highlands and Islands. He had armed himself with paper, ink, pens, one pound of gunpowder, six pounds of shot, flints and bullets, powder-horn and fowling piece, handline and hooks, and a quarter pound of snuff. If he had lived in the days of chivalry, he said, he would have been another Quixote.

His companion on the tour was a James Shand, who wanted to broaden his knowledge of topography and zoology. Not long after setting out on their journey they met a band of tinkers and it looked as if some of their armament might be needed. One of the tinkers, an ex-soldier, looked threatening and MacGillivray and his friend loaded their fowling pieces, but nothing happened.

MacGillivray was accustomed to journeys on foot, but his friend found it hard going. MacGillivray would probably have been quite happy travelling on his own: 'Men who fly from solitude as from a demon,' he said, 'are weak as the ghosts of Ossian.' Their expedition took the two travellers to Poolewe and from there to Stornoway and on to Harris. It was in Harris that MacGillivray's two uncles lived, and it was there that he got his early schooling, walking from the farm of Northtown to the parish school at Obbe.

MacGillivray, who was to become Professor of Natural History at Aberdeen's Marischal College, thought little of his school days. After his death, a poem was found in his papers which showed where his heart really lay:

The solitude of Nature were my school,
And in the moaning voice of streams and winds,
Without the aid of dull scholastic rule,
I felt the tone, which in the lone heart finds its echoes.

When I was stravaiging in the hills I often found myself in places MacGillivray had visited. Halfway up Glen Callater there is supposed to be a green hillock where the 'little folk' lived. Professor MacGillivray reported in 1850 that a man still living had seen fairies dancing on the hillock, with a piper playing to them. Sadly, they didn't make an appearance when I was there.

Lochnagar was one of his haunts. I had always thought of Lochnagar as dark and dour, a mountain to treat with caution. I have a big picture of it hanging on my lounge wall. It was painted by Eric Auld and it is magnificent, but some of my friends say it is too cold for them. William MacGillivray wrote about Lochnagar's 'never-tiring glories'. He said it had more dignity than any of our hills, except Ben Nevis.

There has been a good deal of controversy over the meaning of the word 'Lochnagar'. Some say its is derived from *loch nan gaoir*, the 'loch of

Lochnagar, painted by Eric Auld

sobbing or wailing', although nobody seems to have explained why anyone was sobbing. Others say that it comes from *loch nan gabha,* meaning 'loch of the goats', and there were certainly goats there. William MacGillivray thought it was *lochan-nan-cear,* the little loch of hares, from the many mountain hares on Lochnagar.

MacGillivray climbed it a number of times and never lost his fondness for it. He once said he could gaze at it every day of the year without getting tired. That from a man who had climbed almost every hill in the Cairngorms. I remember standing on the edge of a corrie at Caenlochan Glen, looking down on its 'hanging gardens', and thinking of how this remarkable man had been there a century before, studying the flora and marvelling at the 'superb view all round'.

Wherever I went I seemed to be dogging his footsteps . . . on the hills beyond Ballater, with Mount Keen 'white in the pale rays of the western sun,' up on the ridge of Bein A'an, 'with its long unwaved, but curiously knobbed ridge,' across the brown moors of Glen Gairn, 'where you could hear the shriek of a white owl and the hum of distant waterfalls'.

I found myself chasing him when I went through Glen Tilt, but halfway up the glen I lost him. In 1816, MacGillivray was on his way home from an excursion when he came to Blair Atholl. His aim was to go from there to the source of the Dee and at Blair Lodge he stopped to get directions. The woman there tried to persuade him to stay the night. She said the hills were bleak and dreary and the nearest house was fifteen miles north. But he had promised to be at the source of the Dee by noon next day to meet his friend William Craigie and he said 'all the dragons of darkness' would not prevent him from getting there.

A woman just arrived from Speyside said he should go through Badenoch to get to it, but MacGillivray said he would rely on his map and go east. They all shook their heads when he left. In his *Journal* he explained how he decided to spend the night in a small valley. 'Around me were the black masses of the granite hills,' he wrote, 'rising to heaven like the giant barriers of an enchanted land; above, the cloudless sky, spangled with stars, beneath; a cold bed of turf.'

When morning came he found himself in an amphitheatre formed by bare craggy hills. 'Not a house was to be seen, not even a tree, nor so much as a blade of green grass. Startled by a cry – the scarlet crest and bright eye of a moor-cock suddenly protruded from a tuft of heather. I heard with delight the well-known kok, kok of the "blessed bird" as the Highlanders call him.'

Looking towards Lochnagar from Glen Bardy, near Ballater

He found a rivulet that ran into the Dee and after a seven-mile trudge he came to a hut tenanted by a man named McHardy, who gave him a glass of whisky and some bread and milk. He had found the Dee and later he met his 'best and most beloved friend', William Craigie, in Braemar. The farm where he got his glass of whisky was called Dubrach, or Dubhbhruach, once the home of Peter Grant, the last surviving rebel from the '45 Rebellion.

William MacGillivary never turned his back on his Harris connections. He married Marion MacAskill, the sister of one of his uncle's wives. They had thirteen children, several of whom died in infancy or childhood. Two sons, John and Paul, became eminent in natural science. MacGillivray died in 1852 in his home in Crown Street, Aberdeen. He was buried in Calton Cemetery in Edinburgh, where his wife and two children were interred. Ironically, it was said that his death was caused by the hill that he loved so much, Lochnagar. While climbing there he caught a severe chill from exposure. He never recovered from it.